sew!

Cath Kidston

sew!

Cath Kidston

PHOTOGRAPHY BY PIA TRYDE

Quadrille
PUBLISHING

Introduction

I'm amazed at how many of my friends – of all generations – are now taking up needlework, whether they are sewing on a button, shortening the hems of their jeans or making their own cushion covers. Suddenly, sewing seems to be everywhere!

I was taught how to hand sew as a small child. I embroidered coasters and spectacle cases, which were proudly given away as presents, and I can clearly remember learning how to do blanket stitch. As a teenager I progressed to lessons on the school sewing machine and although it took a whole term to make a towelling dressing gown, my enthusiasm remained undiminished. But many of us don't have the first idea how to set about the rewarding process of creating something from scratch.

The idea for this book came about because I really felt that there was a gap in the market for a collection of inspiring and interesting sewing projects that would include something to suit everybody, whatever their previous experience. If you're an absolute beginner, an experienced stitcher or someone keen to renew rusty skills, Sew! will show you just how to make things yourself – with all the sense of achievement that brings.

If you are like me, you probably don't want to wade through a serious instruction manual but are looking for some practical and clear advice which you'll find in the Sew! Basics section. I also hope to encourage and inspire you at the same time. There are over forty projects in this book which range from old standbys like the covered coat hangers, that can be made in an hour

or so, to more long-term undertakings like the charming patchwork cot quilt. I hope you'll find something that appeals amongst the various napkins, lavender pillows, aprons, cushions and the many different bags, which include a cool iPod holder, a traditional duffel and my favourite new idea, the quirky inside-out tote.

Some of the best fun I had when planning the book was going through my textile archive, choosing precisely which prints and colourways to use for each project. As well as my own designs, there are old and new florals, stripes, ginghams, vintage linen and soft cotton sheeting. You'll see some of my tips on fabric choices as you read through the pages: mix and match patterns, go for detailed embellishments in clashing colours and always try out unexpected combinations. These are your starting points and you can develop and customise the basic designs as you wish. It's up to you how far you want to go and the journey is so rewarding.

With so many ideas included, there is no excuse not to start straightaway! Before long, you'll find you have a sewing project permanently on the go. I've always found getting started is easy: the hard bit is putting it down!

Cath Kidson

Sew! Basics

Essential Equipment

All the fabric and haberdashery needed for each project is detailed in the 'what you will need' lists. One of the last items is always 'sewing kit' – the basic tools required for all your needlework. You may already have many of them, but here's my guide to sewing box essentials.

NEEDLES

There are several types of needle, each designed for a particular task. They come in different lengths and diameters, from a thick '1' to a fine '10' for the most delicate work. Start off with a mixed packet, which will include:

• medium-length 'sharps' with small round eyes for sewing thread. These are for general stitching and tacking.

• 'crewel' needles which have longer eyes to accommodate thicker embroidery cotton. These are easier to thread and fine for hand-sewing too.

• short 'quilting' needles which go easily through several layers of fabric and wadding with a stabbing action.

• a large, blunt tapestry needle or larger bodkin will be useful for threading cords or elastic.

PINS

I always like to use long, slender glass-headed pins, which are not only pretty, but easy to spot against patterned fabric. Keep them in a pincushion or tin, with a magnet close to hand, just in case they spill.

SEWING THREADS

Lustrous No. 50 mercerized sewing cotton is an all-purpose thread for stitching on natural fibres, so it's good for these projects. Match thread to the main colour of your fabric; if this isn't possible, choose a shade darker. Use a contrasting shade for tacking so you can easily unpick the stitches. Use extra strong buttonhole thread for securing upholstered buttons, like those on the floor cushions. If you are going to do a lot of hand quilting, use special quilter's thread.

THIMBLE

Using a thimble for the first time can feel very awkward, but it's worth persevering if you want to avoid punctured fingertips! They come in various sizes, so choose one that fits snugly but not too tightly on your middle finger.

SCISSORS

You will need three basic pairs in three sizes:

• small embroidery scissors with narrow, pointed blades. Use these for snipping buttonholes, trimming threads and clipping curves and corners.

• a pair of medium-sized general purpose scissors for cutting out smaller items and your paper patterns.

• bent-handled dressmaker's shears for accurate fabric cutting. Invest in a good pair with steel blades and don't ever, ever use them for paper!

• pinking shears are also useful, but not essential. They produce a zigzagged edge that reduces fraying on un-neatened seams, and gives a decorative effect on felt.

MEASURING UP

A good tape measure is invaluable. Look out for a strong non-stretchy plastic one with metal tips. A clear ruler, marked with centimetre divisions is very useful when you are marking quilting lines, seams or buttonhole positions.

MARKING TOOLS

Water-soluble or fading ink pens are designed for transferring markings onto fabric, but traditional tailor's chalk or chalk pencils are just as good. Use a light colour on dark fabrics and vice versa. A sharp HB drawing pencil will give a fine, accurate line to guide your quilting.

top tip

MORE USEFUL ITEMS WITH WHICH TO STOCK YOUR WORK BASKET INCLUDE: A NEEDLE-THREADER, A SEAM UNPICKER, A BIG REEL OF WHITE SEWING THREAD, SOME SPARE MACHINE NEEDLES, A CARD OF ELASTIC AND A TIN FOR SPARE BUTTONS, BUCKLES, SAFETY PINS AND OTHER ACCUMULATED BITS AND BOBS.

Sewing Machines

The range of sewing machines that is now on the market can seem a bit bewildering, whether you're a new enthusiast or an old hand who has been stitching for years! There is a huge choice available, from entry-level machines which have no extra gadgets, to highly technical electronic versions with pre-programmed stitches, alphabets and LCDs, that can be linked up to your own computer to create complex embroidery designs.

They may look different, but all have the same basic functions and all you need to make up any of my projects is a solid, functional machine that will give you a regular straight stitch with an even tension.

HOW THEY WORK

All sewing machines work by linking two threads, one above the fabric and one below it, to produce a lock stitch. The upper reel is threaded through the arm of the machine, and down to the needle whilst the lower thread is wound onto a small bobbin. For a straight stitch the needle stays in one central position, but for buttonholes and zigzags it moves from side to side. Original hand machines do not have this swing-needle function, but many are still in working order.

THE PARTS OF THE MACHINE

Take time to read through the manual that comes with your machine. This will have a useful diagram that labels all the various dials and switches: study this carefully and get familiar with the terminology. However complicated the computerised element may be, all machines have the same working parts and structure.

• The **spool pin** sits at the top right of the machine. Slip your reel of sewing cotton onto this and follow the manual's instructions to thread the end through to the needle.

• The **bobbin winder** is also on the top of the machine. This is used for winding thread from the main reel onto the small bobbins that carry the lower thread.

• The **tension adjuster** alters the amount of pressure on the upper thread.

• The **needle** screws into the arm of the machine, just in front of the presser foot. It has a hole at the tip, unlike a sewing needle. There are various sizes: you need a 'universal' or medium size 14/90 for these projects. Remember that the tip must always be sharp, so change needles regularly.

• The **presser foot** maintains pressure on the fabric as it passes under the needle. It lifts up and down with a lever. Your machine will come with several different feet, and many more are available for specialised stitching. Apart from the basic foot, you will need a zip foot which enables you to sew close to piping cord or the teeth of a zip. Other feet are used for hemming, gathering or applying ready-made bias binding.

• The flat **throat plate** has a small hole through which the needle passes to pick up the lower thread. It is marked with a series of parallel lines. Align the edges of your fabric to these as you sew, for a regular seam allowance.

• The **feed dog** is a series of serrated ridges under the throat plate which move up and down to ease the fabric along, as it passes under the presser foot.

• The **bobbin case** is the one working part of the machine that you can't see immediately. It sits under the main bed and houses the bobbin with the lower thread. You can change the tension when necessary by adjusting the small grub screw.

• The **reverse stitch control** is very useful as it enables you to work a few stitches in the opposite direction at the beginning and end of each seam to prevent unravelling.

• The **foot pedal** plugs into the machine and is your speed control. Like a car's accelerator, the harder you press, the faster the machine will go, so take it easy at first.

TENSION

A line of machine stitching should look exactly the same on both sides. Do a sample row before starting work and if you can see a row of loops on one side, there is a problem with the tension. Check your manual and adjust the top or bottom thread as necessary.

 top tip → ALWAYS USE THE SAME THREAD AT THE TOP AND BOTTOM OF THE MACHINE. IT'S A GOOD IDEA TO BUY SOME EXTRA BOBBINS AND FILL THEM BEFORE YOU START ON A NEW PROJECT — THIS WAY YOU CAN CHANGE OVER QUICKLY WHEN THE THREAD RUNS OUT.

Making The Patterns

THE PATTERN SHEET

To download an exclusive pdf of a cleverly designed pattern sheet to help you make all the projects in this book, please go to: **http://www.quadrille.co.uk/pages/sew.**

The pattern sheet shows a series of coloured geometric shapes, which at first glance may seem to be a rather complicated underground map or a circuit diagram. However, look closely and you'll see that each individual outline represents a clearly distinguishable pattern piece, which is marked with a letter from A through to Z and all the way up to PP.

Some of these shapes are one-offs – you'll easily spot 'W', the pattern for the quilted hottie cover and 'T', which is the specs case. Others are multipurpose and are used in two or more projects – for instance, the largest circle 'Y' is the pattern for the top and bottom of the beanie cushion but it also doubles up as a bath hat.

MAKING YOUR OWN PATTERNS

Each of the squares on the pattern sheet indicates 1cm and the shapes include the seam allowance. Buy a pack of dressmaker's squared paper, which is marked with the same 1cm grid as the pattern sheet, and simply copy the pattern pieces onto this, transferring the measurements exactly.

PATTERN MARKINGS

As well as the letters, some of the pieces have an extra broken line drawn across them, which represents an alternative cutting line. The main shape of the oven glove, for instance, is 'U', and line '1u' marks the size of the mitts at each end.

Some of the squares and rectangles have additional broken inner lines, which will give you rounded corners. The instructions will always tell you when to follow these lines.

Other pattern shapes have one side indicated with a dotted line with a double-headed bent arrow pointing towards it. This indicates that the side of the pattern should be placed along folded fabric, to give you a double width or length.

CUTTING OUT GUIDES

Each of the projects has its own cutting out guide. Like the diagram on a dressmaking pattern, this shows you just which pattern pieces you will need and how best to lay them out on your fabric. The fabric quantities in the 'what you will need' shopping list always allow an extra 5cm all round from the minimum amount required, but if you want to match up prints or stripes you will need to buy extra fabric. These guides are shown on a grid, so that you can use them to scale up the shapes if you do not have access to the pdf of the pattern sheet.

FABRIC GRAIN

You'll see that some of the pattern pieces on the cutting out guides are marked with a double-headed arrow, pointing from top to bottom of the page. This indicates the direction of the straight, lengthwise grain of the fabric, which runs parallel to the sides or selvedges. The cross grain – the bias – runs diagonally across the fabric and has a certain amount of 'give'. Some of the pieces, such as binding strips, have to be cut on the bias so that they will stretch.

top tip

TRANSFER ALL THE MARKINGS, INCLUDING THE LETTERS, TO YOUR PATTERN PIECES BEFORE YOU CUT THEM OUT. KEEP THE PIECES FOR EACH PROJECT TOGETHER IN LARGE LABELLED ENVELOPES SO THAT YOU WILL BE ABLE TO REUSE THEM AT A FUTURE DATE.

Hems & Edges

A raw edge can be neatened in two ways: either by turning it back and stitching it down to make a hem, or by binding it with a narrow strip of fabric.

A single hem, with just one turning, is used for dressmaking and soft furnishings. Most of the projects require a double hem, which has two turnings. This gives a firmer edge, which is often top-stitched. The depth of the turnings will always be given in the step-by-step instructions.

A bound hem gives a very professional finish, especially if you use a contrasting fabric. You can buy bias binding – a narrow pre-folded strip of plain cotton – in a range of colours and two widths, or make your own from a co-ordinating print.

SINGLE HEM
Firstly, zigzag the edge of the fabric. With the wrong side facing, fold the edge up to the given measurement. You can use a ruler to make sure the hem is a consistent depth. Pin the turning, then tack it if you wish, and machine stitch, just below the neatened edge.

DOUBLE HEM
Fold and press the first turning to the required depth, then make the second turning, as directed. The first turning is usually shorter, but sometimes they are both equal. Pin and tack in place, then either machine stitch close to the inner fold or slip stitch by hand. Top stitch the outer fold on a pocket.

BOUND STRAIGHT EDGES
Open out one edge of the binding and, with right sides facing, pin it to the edge of the fabric. Machine stitch along the first fold. Turn the binding over to the wrong side and tack it down close to the fold. Finish by slip stitch as for the curved corner, or machine stitch on the right side, just inside the edge of the binding.

BOUND CURVES

A bound curve on a single layer of fabric needs to be reinforced with stay-stitch – a row of machine stitching worked about 4mm from the edge – to prevent it curling inwards. With right sides facing, tack the edge of the binding along the curve. Gather it in slightly so that the centre fold will fit comfortably around the outside edge without pulling.

Fold the rest of the binding to the back and sew down the edge by hand or machine. You may find that it helps to steam press the curve along the folded edge of the binding before you stitch.

MAKING YOUR OWN BINDING

For a straight edge, you can cut the fabric strips along the grain of the fabric, but for a curved edge they should be on the bias. Trim the ends diagonally, at 45 degrees. To join two strips, pin together with the right sides facing and the ends overlapping as shown. Seam between the points where they cross.

Press the seams open and trim off the projecting triangles. Fold the strip in half lengthways, with wrong sides together and press. Press each edge in turn towards the centre fold.

Seams

Joining two pieces of fabric is the most basic of all sewing techniques, and if you can do it neatly and accurately, you're ready to create any of the projects in this book!

Careful preparation pays off, and if you are new to sewing, it's worth tacking your seams together once they are pinned. This temporary stitch holds the fabric in place as you machine stitch, and is more stable than pins alone. Use a contrasting thread and sew with long running stitches, just inside the seam line.

When you're making an item that will be laundered or that will undergo heavy wear, it's a good idea to neaten the edges with a zigzag or binding, either before you join the seam or afterwards.

STRAIGHT SEAM

Pin the two pieces together with right sides facing and the edges aligned. Stitch along the given seam allowance, using the footplate lines as a width guide. Reinforce each end with a few extra stitches and press the allowance open or to one side, as directed.

CORNER SEAM

When you reach a corner, keep the needle down and lift the presser foot. Turn the fabric and continue along the next edge. Trim the allowance, to within 2mm of the stitch line. Turn right side out and gently ease the corner into shape with a blunt pencil.

T-JUNCTION SEAM

This seam is used to give width to bags. Join the side and bottom seams and press open. Refold the open corner so that the ends of the seams are aligned. Pin the two sides together and stitch. Trim the allowance and bind or zigzag to neaten.

CURVED SEAMS

Trim the allowance back to 6mm so that the seam will not be too bulky. For outside curves, like the top of a heart, cut out a series of regularly spaced little notches to within 2mm of the stitch line. For inside curves, make a series of snips at right angles to the stitching.

CLOSING A GAP

Sometimes you'll need to leave a gap in a seam through which to add the filling. Press back the seam allowance on each side before turning right side out. Pin the two edges together and slip stitch, passing the needle through the edges of the folds for an unobtrusive finish.

TOP STITCHING

Use this to secure folded edges or to reinforce a seam. On a fold, stitch 3mm in from the edge using the presser foot opening as a guide. For a straight or curved seam, press the allowance to one side, then stitch through all three layers from the right side, 3mm from the join.

CIRCULAR SEAM

Cut 6mm notches around the circle and 1cm slits at the end of the fabric tube, spacing them 2cm apart. Fold the circle and tube four times so you have eight equal divisions and mark the ends of the folds. Pin together, right sides facing, matching the marks. Tack just inside the seam line, then machine with the circle on top.

PIPED SEAM

Piping – a tube of fabric–covered cord sewn between the two layers – defines a seam visually. Cut a narrow bias strip and fold it around a length of cord with wrong sides facing. Tack close to the cord and unpick any visible tacking once the seam is completed.

Fastenings

A visit to your local haberdashers or needlework supplier will show you just how many different types of fastenings exist. Some of these you may have already used when making clothes or soft furnishings: press-studs, hooks and eyes, fabric-covered buttons and zips, whilst others are designed specifically for homeware and accessories, such as magnetic bag fasteners and spring toggles.

I always love to add extra detail by using traditional hand-sewing techniques, and the buttonhole stitch loops used on the specs case and quilted purse are my current favourites. I used tailored rouleau loops for the hottie and shoulder bag. Handmade buttonholes, also worked in tailor's buttonhole stitch, give individual character to the shoulder bag strap and the large tote – and the effort and patience involved in creating them will pay off in the end!

BUTTONS

Although I've used them to fasten most of the bags and cases in this book, buttons have many other decorative purposes. Fabric-covered buttons are ideal for upholstering cushions, and I've used shirt buttons as the finishing touch on the lavender pillow, and as eyes for the various appliqué birds and the Stanley toy. Scour antique and charity shops for one-off examples, salvage them from old garments and sort through the family button tin to find vintage examples in pressed glass, painted plastic, metal, wood or lustrous mother-of-pearl.

HANDMADE BUTTONHOLE

Draw a line, the same size as your button, along the grain of the fabric. Reinforce it with two lines of back stitches. Carefully cut along the line. Using a long length of stranded cotton, sew a round of tailor's buttonhole stitch around the slit, curving each end. Stitch from right to left, inserting the needle upwards, then pulling it back towards you so that the looped thread forms a small knot at the base of each stitch.

BUTTONHOLE STITCH LOOP

This is also worked in stranded thread. Fasten on at the edge of the fabric and make a foundation bar of three or four loose stitches. Starting from the right, work tailor's buttonhole stitch over the threads, looping the thread twice under the needle as shown. Fasten off at the left.

ROULEAU LOOP

A rouleau is a narrow flexible tube, made from a bias strip of fabric. Fold the strip in half and stitch about 3mm from the fold, slanting the end of the seam out to the corner. Trim back the seam allowance to 3mm. Thread a tapestry needle with strong thread, fasten it to the corner and tie the ends together. Pass the needle carefully through the tube so that the fabric is gradually turned right side out.

ZIPS

This is a quick method for inserting a zip into a seam. Press back a 2cm turning along each edge, then tack the two folds loosely together. Tack the closed zip securely to the wrong side, so that the teeth lie exactly along the join. Fit a zip foot and sew the zip in place 6mm from the outside edge of the teeth. Stitch three times across the top and bottom edges at right angles. Unpick the tacking.

Ties & Handles

Ties and handles can be viewed as purely functional aspects of a design – the means by which you carry a bag, for example – but in fact they provide a great opportunity to add extra detailing, such as a splash of contrasting colour or a new texture.

You can buy some interesting ready-made handles, like the cane loops bound with scarlet twine that I hunted down for the knitting bag, but you easily can make your own from folded and stitched strips of fabric. A similar construction technique is used for apron ties and these are particularly effective when a plain colour is used alongside a print: take a look at the cowboy apron on page 90.

TWO-PART HANDLE
The button-on strap for the shoulder bag has rounded ends, and so I made it from two pieces of fabric. These were sewn together with a gap left in the seam, then turned right side out and top stitched. A similar strap with square ends could be made by the folded handle method opposite, which is more straightforward.

REINFORCING STITCHING
Give additional strength to the ends of your handle with reinforcing stitching. Machine stitch a square or rectangle, then sew diagonal lines between the corners.

WEBBING
Webbing is a sturdy woven tape, which you can find in subtle natural cotton colours or more vivid nylon shades. It comes in widths from around 2cm to 8cm. I used a 4cm webbing to make the handle on the shopper bag, stitching the two edges together along the centre, so it is easier to grip.

FOLDED HANDLE OR TIE

Press the strip in half lengthways with right sides facing, then press the sides to the centre. Tack, then top stitch the two edges to make a strong, open-ended strap. You can sew the ends together to make a looped handle. To mitre the ends, fold and press each corner inwards at 45 degrees before pressing in the sides. Press the end triangles inwards.

NARROW TIES

The washbag's stylish ties are made from long rouleaux. Dressmakers use a thin latchet hook to turn these through, but you can use the method on page 25. Pull the needle slowly, so the fabric doesn't get jammed. The jewellery roll ties are a cheat's way of making a similar fabric tie: simply slip stitch together the folded edges of a length of bias binding.

CORD

I chose a soft woven cotton cord for the duffel bag. Piping cord, which would work equally well, is twisted and a little firmer. It comes in various thicknesses from around 4 to 12m. The iPod case has a drawstring made from the narrow nylon cord used for Roman blinds. You'll find both this and piping cord at furnishing suppliers.

Appliqué & Quilting

Appliqué – creating designs from cut out fabric shapes – is a great way to use up all kinds of scraps and offcuts. I like to work with Bondaweb, the quickest way to trace and fix down the motifs, but tried out a more traditional technique for the bird cushion. The full-size trace-off templates are on pages 155–160. Remember that you may need to reverse these outlines, as iron-on appliqué always gives you a mirror image of the original template.

IRON-ON APPLIQUE
Read the manufacturer's instructions before starting work, and check the heat setting on your iron. Use a pressing cloth if you are working with felt.

1 Trace the outlines onto the paper side of the Bondaweb with a pencil. Cut them out roughly, leaving a small margin around each shape.

2 Place the motifs onto the wrong side of the fabric, with the paper upwards, fitting them together like a jigsaw. Press down with a dry iron.

3 Cut each shape out around the outline. Peel off the papers and position them on the background fabric, adhesive downwards. Press in place.

EDGING THE MOTIFS
Edging each element with a round of stitching is both practical and decorative: it prevents any fraying and adds extra definition to the shapes.

STRAIGHT STITCH
You can finish each motif by hand with small straight stitches worked at right angles to the edge in sewing cotton or stranded embroidery thread.

ZIGZAG
An open zigzag, machined in plain white, gives a hardwearing finish to items that will need to be laundered.

SATIN STITCH
A narrow satin stitch edging is the most functional of all. Match the sewing thread to the colours of the felt.

TURNED-EDGE APPLIQUE

Start off by tracing or photocopying the motif and cut out each separate element from paper. You can use the paper templates several times.

1 Pin the template to your fabric with wrong sides upwards. Cut out leaving a 4mm allowance, then fold this margin over and tack down.

2 Press to set the fold and unpick the papers. Pin the shape in position and slip stitch the folded edge to the background.

3 For a raised effect, gently push a small amount of polyester filling under the shape before stitching it down.

QUILTING

Quilting gives a raised, padded look to fabric and the technique can be as sophisticated as the padded purse on page 130 or as cosy as a hottie cover. Simply sandwich a piece of cotton batting or polyester wadding between your main fabric and a backing fabric, and stitch all three layers together.

For a diamond pattern, use a clear ruler, a set square and a sharp pencil to mark a grid across the surface of your fabric. Tack the three layers together securely and stitch along the pencil lines using a short quilting needle.

Decorative Details

If you love textiles as much as I do, you are sure to have your own hoard of trimmings, stored away and awaiting a new lease of life. Used with discretion, lace, braid or ricrac can provide the perfect detail that completes a project and adds a personal touch.

A narrow border of crisp white lace will enhance a sprigged floral print, and always looks great with its natural partner, vintage linen. Try an edging of primary coloured ricrac or a ribbon bow to bring out the brighter tones within a fabric design, and if you can't get a precise match, follow my example and go for a gloriously clashing contrast. You can add accents of colour with velvet bows, but sometimes a simple bias binding or cotton tape will work just as well. Good haberdashery departments and specialist stores have an enticing array of new trimmings, and you can easily find vintage lace and ribbons at flea markets, antique dealers and even charity shops if you persevere and if you enjoy a good rummage.

Embroidery is another effective way to add colour and fine detail, such as the cowboy lassos on the boy's apron or Stan's name on his dog tag. Hanks of stranded cotton threads come in a rainbow of colours. Use all six strands and a long-eyed needle for bold stitches, and a few threads and a finer needle for more delicate work.

HAND STITCHES

Most of the projects in the book are sewn by machine, but you'll find that they also involve a few hand and embroidery techniques. Most of these are explained in the step-by-step instructions, but here are a few other basic stitches, which you may find useful.

RUNNING STITCH

This is worked on a large scale when you are tacking or gathering, and on a smaller scale for hand quilting. The spaces and the stitches should always be a consistent length.

BACK STITCH

Use this for hand seaming on small projects and for 'writing'. Take the needle backwards and down through the fabric, then bring it back up one stitch length ahead of the first stitch.

CHAIN STITCH

This gives you a broad, flexible line. Loop the thread under the point of the needle from left to right before you pull it through, then take the needle back down through the loop of the last stitch.

RICRAC

There's something very appealing about ricrac braid – it always looks cheerful and comes in wonderful colours. If you set it into a seam or under a turned back hem, you get a little row of scallops peeping out. I used bright red ricrac to trim the rosebud egg cosies and a broader, more subtle yellow to edge the flap of the quilted purse.

LACE

Border lace has one straight and one curvy edge. Work a row of running stitches along the straight edge and pull up the thread if you want a gathered effect, or leave it flat for a plainer look. The torchon lace I used on the lavender pillow was a lucky find from my local sewing shop. For the bath hat I used a narrower and more practical broderie anglaise with a pre-gathered edge.

RIBBON

The double-face velvet ribbon used to embellish the pincushion was a bit of an extravagance, but as I only needed a short length it was worth splashing out for a luxurious finishing touch. Remember that there's more to ribbon than just bows however: the tablecloth is edged with red and white gingham ribbon that is an exact match for the appliqué fabric.

Sew! Projects

The challenge I set for myself with this book was to design projects that were practical as well as pretty. I selected a variety of items that cover all the basic sewing skills and added in some decorative details. Combing through my fabric archives to find the perfect print for each one was so much fun; the best possible inspiration to pick up a sewing needle and thread!

Square Cushion

SKILL LEVEL

Ticking stripes and pretty floral prints always complement each other, so mix and match the two fabrics to create this deceptively simple cushion. It's an ideal starter project and to make things really easy there's no need to stitch any buttonholes – simply snip off the buttons when the cover needs to be laundered.

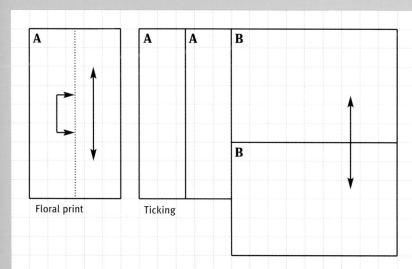

Floral print Ticking

cutting out

Centre front: Cut 1 x A from floral print, on the fold
Side fronts: Cut 2 x A from striped fabric
Back panels: Cut 2 x B from striped fabric

The seam allowance throughout is 1.5cm

1 With right sides facing, sew the side fronts to the long edges of the centre front. Press the seams open.

2 Hem the top edge of the bottom back panel by pressing under 1cm, then a further 4cm. Pin and stitch down. Neaten the lower edge of the top back panel in the same way.

3 Position the cushion front and bottom back panel together, with right sides facing, lining up the raw edges. Lay the top panel in place, again matching the edges.

4 Pin the three pieces together, then sew around all four sides. Clip the corners (see page 22) and turn the cover right side out. Press lightly.

5 Insert the pad and fasten the cover by sewing the buttons securely through both panels, 2cm down from the edge and 12.5cm in from the corners.

top tip → DEPENDING ON THE WIDTH OF THE PATTERN REPEAT, YOU MAY NEED TO ALLOW EXTRA TICKING TO ENSURE THAT THE TWO SIDE FRONTS ARE SYMMETRICAL. LINE UP BOTH BACK PANELS CAREFULLY WHEN CUTTING OUT, SO THAT THE STRIPES WILL MATCH ACROSS THE OPENING.

Bolster Cushion

what you will need...

- 85 x 55cm floral print cotton
- 2 x 4cm self-cover buttons
- matching sewing thread
- buttonhole thread
- sewing kit
- sewing machine
- 50cm bolster cushion pad with 18cm diameter

SKILL LEVEL

There's something about a feather-filled bolster that adds a little boudoir luxury to any setting, and the cylindrical shape makes an impact whether on its own or piled alongside an assortment of other cushions. Don't be put off by the circular seams – you'll find clear instructions for this on page 23.

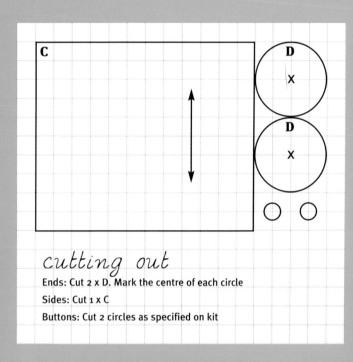

cutting out

Ends: Cut 2 x D. Mark the centre of each circle

Sides: Cut 1 x C

Buttons: Cut 2 circles as specified on kit

1 Press back a 1cm turning along each short edge of the main piece.

2 With right sides facing, pin these two edges at the corners. Slip stitch the front and back folds together for 5cm at each end, leaving a long opening between them.

3 Find the centre of each end piece by folding the circles into quarters and mark this point. Following the diagram and steps on page 23, sew one to each end of the main piece with a 1.5cm seam.

4 Turn the cover right side out and ease the circular seams into shape. Insert the cushion pad through the side opening.

5 Gather up the outside edge of each small circle and slip them over the domed tops of the self-cover buttons. Tighten the threads, then clip on the backings as directed by the manufacturer.

6 Pass a length of buttonhole thread through one of the button shanks and thread both ends through the eye of a large, long needle.

7 Plunge the needle through both the cover and the bolster at the marked centre point, then bring the needle out through the side of the bolster. Pull the thread up tightly and fasten off securely.

8 Pin the edges of the opening together and slip stitch the two folds to complete the cover.

top → *tip*

I CHOSE A VINTAGE FRENCH ROSE PRINT FOR MY CUSHION, BUT YOU CAN OPT FOR A MORE FORMAL LOOK BY USING TICKING, CUT SO THE STRIPES RUN EITHER LENGTHWAYS OR AROUND THE COVER. THE TRADITIONAL WAY TO FINISH A BOLSTER IS WITH A CONTRASTING ROUND OF PIPING AT EACH END.

Bird Cushion

SKILL LEVEL

You'll find these dear little birds popping up in different guises throughout the book! Here I've used the motif in both sizes to make a whole family in turned-edge appliqué, complete with padded wings. The combination of yellow ricrac, crisp spots and ditsy flowers gives a spring-like freshness to the design.

what you will need...

- 50 x 20cm white cotton fabric
- 50 x 60cm floral print cotton
- tracing paper and pencil
- 15cm square blue spotted fabric
- 15cm square pink spotted fabric
- polyester toy filling
- 2 small buttons
- 2 black seed beads
- green stranded embroidery cotton
- 1m 12mm-wide ricrac
- matching sewing thread
- sewing kit
- sewing machine
- 30 x 45cm cushion pad

E

White cotton

F

F

E

E

Floral print

cutting out

Centre front: Cut 1 x E from white cotton

Top and bottom front: Cut 2 x F from floral print

Back panels: Cut 2 x E from floral print

templates

Small bird and Mini bird, page 159

1 Following the steps on page 29, make up the body and wing pieces for the four birds, reversing two of them. Sew the bodies to the centre front. Add the beads to the small birds and the buttons to the large birds for eyes.

2 Stitch a length of ricrac to the top and bottom of the centre front, so that the curves just touch the edge of the fabric. Pin the top and bottom fronts in place, with right sides facing.

3 Machine stitch the seams 6mm from the edge. Carefully press so that the ricrac curves point outwards and the seam allowances lie inwards. Embroider the green grass with a few lines of straight stitch.

4 Hem one long edge of each back panel. Place the cushion front right side upwards, then position the back panels along the top and bottom, with raw edges aligned. Pin together and seam all four sides, 1cm from the edge.

5 Clip the corners and turn the cover right side out. Insert the cushion pad and slip stitch the opening to close.

top tip → IF YOU CAN'T FIND THE RIGHT SIZE PAD, YOU CAN QUICKLY MAKE YOUR OWN BESPOKE FILLING FROM TWO RECTANGLES OF CALICO CUT 2CM LARGER ALL ROUND THAN THE FINISHED COVER. JOIN WITH A 1CM SEAM, TURN THROUGH, AND STUFF WITH POLYESTER WADDING. SLIP STITCH TO CLOSE.

Floor Cushions

what you will need...

- 140 x 90cm floral print cotton duck
- 50 x 50 x 10cm foam cushion pad
- 5 x 2.5cm self-cover buttons
- 5 x 2.5cm buttons
- buttonhole thread
- upholstery needle
- matching sewing thread
- sewing kit
- sewing machine

SKILL LEVEL

Long summer days are just made for outdoor living and these thick, square cushions will ensure your creature comforts whether you're at a festival, picnicking, camping, or simply lounging about in the garden. You'll need a specially long and strong upholstery needle to secure the buttons that give them their special padded look.

I x 10

cutting out

Front and back: Cut 2 x G

Sides: Cut 4 x H

Tufts: Cut 10 x I

Buttons: Cut 5 circles as specified on kit

top tip → GETTING THE BUTTONS TO SINK RIGHT BACK INTO THE FOAM FILLING ACTUALLY TAKES QUITE A BIT OF EFFORT, SO BE PREPARED TO WORK HARD! SEE IF YOU CAN RECRUIT A FRIEND TO HELP PUSH THE PAD DOWN ON EITHER SIDE OF THE BUTTON POSITIONS AS YOU PULL THE THREAD.

Floor Cushions

1 Mark the 5 button positions on the front and back pieces, one at the centre and four points 20cm diagonally in from each corner.

2 Pin the long edge of the first side to one edge of the front piece. Starting and finishing the seam 1.5cm in from the raw edges, machine stitch together with a 1.5cm seam. Join the other three sides to the front in the same way.

3 Now pin and stitch the short edges of all four sides together to make a shallow box. Seam each edge from the point where it meets the front to 1.5cm from the corner.

4 Carefully trim a small triangle of fabric from all three pieces at each corner.

5 Pin and stitch three edges of the front panel to the 'box' in the same way and clip the corners.

6 Turn the cover right side out and press under a 1.5cm turning along the two open edges. Insert the cushion pad and pin the folded edges together. Slip stitch from corner to corner.

7 Cover the buttons as directed. Fold two tuft strips into loops, overlapping the ends by 2cm, then cross one over the other. Thread 50cm of buttonhole thread through a button and pass both ends through the upholstery needle. Plunge the needle into the front of the cushion at a marked point.

8 Push the needle right through the pad, bringing it out at the corresponding mark on the back. Pass the ends of the thread through the holes in a plain button. Pull up tightly so that the buttons sink into the pad. Knot and trim the ends. Add the other buttons in the same way.

top tip

HIGH DENSITY SEATING FOAM CAN BE ORDERED FROM SPECIALIST SUPPLIERS, WHO WILL CUT IT TO THE EXACT SIZE AND DEPTH REQUIRED. ASK FOR A STOCKINETTE WRAP, WHICH SOFTENS THE EDGES, PROTECTS THE FOAM AND MAKES IT EASIER TO GET THE PAD INSIDE YOUR COVER.

Flower Cushion

what you will need...

- 35 x 55cm white cotton fabric
- 50 x 80cm red cotton fabric
- selection of floral print scraps
- bondaweb
- pencil
- matching sewing threads
- sewing kit
- sewing machine
- 35 x 50cm cushion pad

SKILL LEVEL

All stitchers are magpies at heart and inevitably acquire an eclectic ragbag, bulging with remnants, offcuts and fabric salvaged from old garments. In a spirit of 'make do and mend' I chose some of my favourite vintage prints to appliqué this red, blue and white cushion: a great way to utilise even the tiniest scraps.

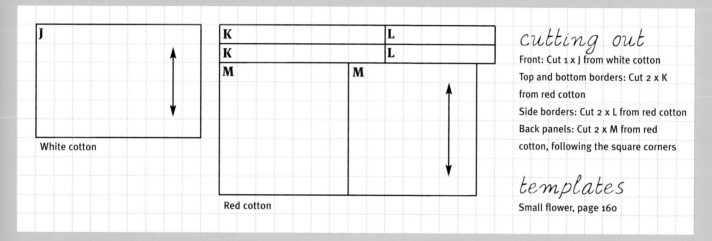

J

White cotton

K | L
K | L
M | M

Red cotton

cutting out

Front: Cut 1 x J from white cotton

Top and bottom borders: Cut 2 x K from red cotton

Side borders: Cut 2 x L from red cotton

Back panels: Cut 2 x M from red cotton, following the square corners

templates

Small flower, page 160

The seam allowance throughout is 1cm

1 Decide which two fabrics to use for each motif. I alternated contrasting red and blue flowers so that the outlines stand out clearly where they overlap.

2 Following the inner outlines, trace twenty ovals (two lots of six petals for the daisies, plus eight leaves), two small circles for the daisy centres, two flower heads and four stalks onto Bondaweb. Cut out and iron onto the prints.

3 Iron down each complete motif in turn, starting at the right and working towards the left. Edge each shape with straight stitch.

4 Trim 6cm from one short edge of J, so it measures 39cm.

5 Stitch a side border to each side edge of the front and press the seams outwards. Add the top and bottom borders, again pressing the seams outwards.

6 Make a 1cm double hem along one side edge of each back panel. Lay out the completed front with the right side facing upwards and place one panel, right side down, across each side, so that the hems overlap in the centre.

7 Pin the three pieces together and machine stitch around all four sides. Clip the corners, turn right side out and press.

8 Insert the pad through the opening. Instead of buying a pad, you can make one from two 37 x 52cm rectangles of calico: see the 'top tip' for the Bird Cushion on page 40.

top tip

TO MAKE SURE THAT THE MOTIFS ARE EVENLY SPACED, LAY ALL THE PIECES OUT ON THE CUSHION FRONT BEFORE YOU REMOVE THE BACKING PAPERS AND MARK THEIR POSITIONS WITH A FADING PEN. ALLOW A 2CM BORDER AT THE SIDES AND 4CM ALONG THE TOP AND BOTTOM EDGES.

Padded Placemats

what you will need...

- 35 x 85cm laundered cotton duck
- 30 x 40cm pre-shrunk cotton wadding
- matching sewing thread
- sewing kit
- ruler
- sewing machine

SKILL LEVEL

Placemats are on the list of useful items that everybody needs at some time, whether it's to protect a polished wooden surface or to add colour to a table setting. Make your own from fabric that co-ordinates with your cutlery, crockery and glassware, and you'll find that every mealtime takes on a festive air.

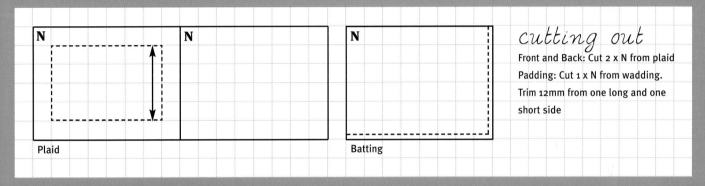

Plaid

Batting

cutting out

Front and Back: Cut 2 x N from plaid

Padding: Cut 1 x N from wadding.

Trim 12mm from one long and one short side

1 Use a fading pen and a ruler to mark a rectangle, 5cm in from the edge, on the right side of the front panel. Pin the padding the wrong side of this panel, centring it so that there is a 5mm margin all round. Tack it in place.

2 Now pin the back panel to the front panel with right sides facing, so that the front panel is sandwiched between the padding and the back.

3 Machine stitch the three layers of fabric and padding together, leaving a 20cm gap along the centre of the bottom edge. Sew 5mm from the edge, so that the stitches run just outside the edge of the wadding.

4 Press back the seam allowance along each side of the opening, clip the corners and turn the placemat right sides out through the gap (see page 22). Tack the opening, making sure the seam allowances lie flat, and slip stitch to close.

5 Machine stitch along the marked line on the front using thread to match or contrast with the main fabric. Finish off with a round of top stitch, 3mm from the outside edge.

top tip

IF YOU USE A PLAID OR CHECK DESIGN AS I DID, SIMPLY FOLLOW THE GEOMETRIC GRID PATTERN TO CUT OUT YOUR MATS AND AS A GUIDE FOR THE RECTANGULAR STITCHING. REMEMBER TO ALLOW EXTRA FABRIC IF YOU WISH TO CENTRE THE PATTERN OR IF YOU ARE GOING TO MAKE A MATCHING SET.

Floral Napkins

what you will need...

- 45cm square floral print
- 60 x 30cm toning plaid or check
- matching sewing thread
- sewing kit
- sewing machine

SKILL LEVEL

The final touch for your table setting has to be a set of napkins. Here I've picked the painterly 'Rose' print on a powder blue background and bordered it with 'Woven Check', the plaid design used for the mats, to show how two mismatched fabrics can look stunning together if they share a colour scheme.

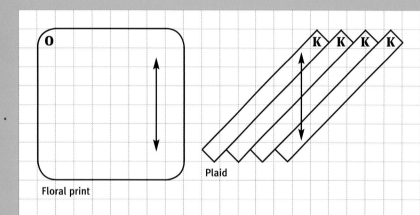

O

Floral print

K K K K

Plaid

cutting out

Napkin: Cut 1 x O from floral print, following the rounded corners

Binding: Cut 4 x K from plaid, on the bias

1 Join the four bias strips at the short ends, overlapping the points as shown on page 21. Press the seams open and trim the points in line with the straight edges. Trim the ends at right angles.

2 Press the binding in half widthways, along the entire length, then press under a 5cm turning at one long edge.

3 Stay stitch the corners of the napkin.

4 Starting in the centre of one side, pin and tack the unpressed binding edge around the napkin, right sides facing. Ease the binding around the corners as on page 21.

5 Trim the end of the binding at a right angle when you have completed the round, allowing a 2cm overlap. Press under 5mm at the loose end and tack in place.

6 Turn the other edge of the binding back to the wrong side of the napkin, so that the raw edge is enclosed, and tack down the fold. Finish off by slip stitching the fold in place.

top tip →

OLD-FASHIONED ETIQUETTE DEMANDED NAPKINS IN A RANGE OF SIZES, FROM DAINTY 30CM SQUARES FOR AFTERNOON TEA UP TO ENORMOUS STARCHED DAMASK VERSIONS FOR FORMAL DINNERS. MAKE YOURS IN THE SIZE THAT SUITS YOU BEST, ENLARGING THE 45CM SQUARE IF NECESSARY.

Heart Teatowel

what you will need...

• 65 x 80cm white linen
• 25 x 65cm floral dress print
• 20cm squares of 6 floral prints
• bondaweb
• matching sewing thread
• sewing kit
• sewing machine

template

Large heart, page 157

SKILL LEVEL

Ditsy floral fabrics always muddle along, side by side, if you keep the patterns on the same scale. I cut six large hearts, each from a different print, to create the iron-on appliqué borders for this teatowel, and edged each one with a round of machine zigzag so that they'll stand up to the daily drying routine.

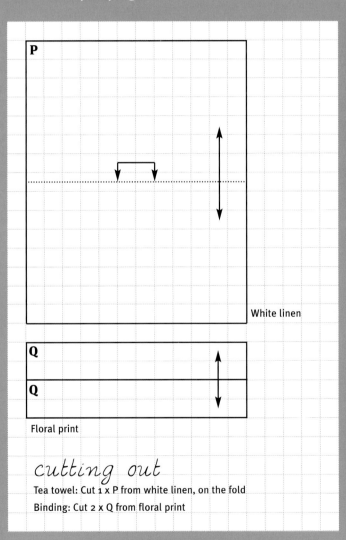

P

White linen

Q

Q

Floral print

cutting out

Tea towel: Cut 1 x P from white linen, on the fold
Binding: Cut 2 x Q from floral print

1 Pin one binding strip, right side down, to each short side of the linen. Machine stitch, 1cm from the edge and press the seam allowances outwards.

2 Press and pin a 1cm double hem along each long side. Top stitch, 3mm from the inside fold.

3 Press under 1cm along the raw edge of both bindings. Turn this to the wrong side and press so that the folds lie just beyond the stitch line. Pin and top stitch from the right side. Slip stitch the open side edges.

4 Trace six hearts onto Bondaweb. Following the technique on page 28, iron each one onto a different fabric. Cut them out and peel off the backing papers.

5 Fold the teatowel in half widthways to find the centre. Position one heart centrally at each end, with the points 1cm away from the binding strips.

6 Iron in place, then add another two hearts at each end, leaving a 2.5cm space on either side of the first motif. Press down. Using white thread, zigzag around each heart by machine.

top tip → OLD LINEN TABLECLOTHS AND SHEETS HAVE A WONDERFULLY SOFT QUALITY THAT ONLY COMES FROM DECADES OF USE AND LAUNDERING. NOT ALL OF THEM SURVIVE INTACT HOWEVER, SO MAKING ONE-OFF TEATOWELS IS A GOOD WAY TO RECYCLE THE BEST PARTS OF THE FABRIC.

Half Apron

what you will need...

- 45 x 130cm cotton duck
- 2m 2cm-wide bias binding
- matching sewing thread
- sewing kit
- sewing machine

SKILL LEVEL

You can brighten up the most mundane household and gardening chores with this practical half-apron: its three pockets are just the right size for dusters or secateurs and twine. Select a vivid floral print for maximum cheerfulness and trim the edges with bias binding in an even stronger colour.

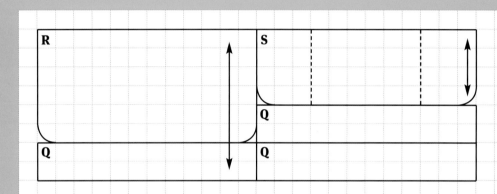

cutting out

Apron: Cut 1 x R

Pocket: Cut 1 x S. Mark a line 15cm from each short side

Ties: Cut 3 x Q

1 Following the directions on page 20, neaten the top edge of the pocket with bias binding. Mark the centre point of this edge. Pin the side and bottom edges to the main apron, matching the rounded corners, and machine stitch, leaving a seam allowance of 6mm.

2 To mark the pocket divisions, rule a line 15cm in from each side edge. Sew the two layers together along both lines.

3 Bind the side and bottom edges, referring to the technique for curved corners on page 21.

4 Join the short ends of the three ties to form one long strip and press the seams open. Press in half lengthways and unfold. Now fold both long edges to the centre crease and press in place. Mitre the short ends (see page 27). Open out the centre fold and fold the strip in half lengthways to find the centre point.

5 Matching up the two centre points, pin the apron to the strip so that the raw top edge lies along the crease. Pin and tack the top edge of the apron to the lower half of the strip.

6 Turn the upper half of the strip over the top edge of the apron and tack it down. Tack the top and bottom halves of the loose ends together to make the left and right ties. Top stitch 3mm all the way along the short and long edges of the strip.

top tip →

APRON POCKETS ALWAYS GET THE MOST WEAR AT THE TOP CORNERS, SO WORK A FEW EXTRA REINFORCING STITCHES AT THE TOP END OF THE DIVIDING LINES AND AT THE POINTS WHERE THE TOP CORNERS OF THE POCKET PIECE MEETS THE MAIN APRON.

Egg Cosy

what you will need...

- 15 x 20cm floral print
- 15 x 20cm felt
- 20cm ricrac
- matching sewing thread
- sewing kit
- sewing machine

SKILL LEVEL

No breakfast tray is complete without a couple of boiled eggs and plate of 'soldiers'. These jolly cosies are made from a rose print and lined with green felt to keep the eggs toasty warm. The curved seams are machine stitched, but this project is also a good way for practising some basic hand stitching.

Floral print   1t

Felt

drawing up the pattern

Cosy: Use piece T with line 1t as the bottom edge

Tab: Use piece I, with line 1i as the right edge

cutting out

Cosy: Cut 2 from floral print

Lining: Cut 2 from felt

Tab: Cut 1 from felt

1 Fold one cosy piece in half widthways to find the centre line. Fold the tab in half lengthways and tack it centrally along the crease, on the right side, so that the two ends line up with the top edge.

2 Pin the second cosy piece over the first, with right sides facing. Stitch the side and top edges together, with a 5mm seam. Clip a series of notches from the curved part of the seam allowance, spacing them 1cm apart (see page 23).

3 Turn the cosy right side out, ease the seam into position and press lightly.

4 Pin the two felt linings together, and stitch 5mm from the side and top edges. Trim the seam allowance back to 3mm.

5 Slip the lining inside the cosy and line up the open edges. Turn them both up together to make a 5mm hem around the opening. Tack in place.

6 Fold the hem up once again. Starting at the centre back, slip the ricrac behind the turning so that the scallops peep out over the top edge. Trim the ends and tuck them under the hem. Tack through all the layers, then stitch the top edge down.

top tip →

WHEN YOU ARE CHOOSING TRIMMINGS AND BINDINGS, PICK OUT ONE OR MORE KEY COLOURS FROM THE PRINTED FABRIC. THIS BRIGHT GREEN FELT IS AN EXACT MATCH FOR THE ROSEBUD STEMS AND LEAVES WHILST THE RED RICRAC IS THE SAME COLOUR AS THE DARKEST PETALS.

Birdie Tablecloth

SKILL LEVEL

Long refectory tables require extra large tablecloths, which aren't always easy to find, so I created this one-off cover by giving a new lease of life to an antique linen sheet. I added an iron-on appliqué border of large hearts and birds cut from two colours of gingham and a toning floral print. The matching edging, made from gingham ribbon, is a speedy and effective way to finish off the cloth. You could use the small-scale versions of these motifs to embellish a set of napkins to go with the tablecloth.

what you will need...

- plain tablecloth or sheet
- for each heart and bird repeat:
  2 20cm gingham squares
  20 x 25cm floral print
  2 small buttons
- bondaweb
- matching sewing thread
- sewing kit
- gingham ribbon to fit around edge of cloth, plus 5cm
- sewing machine

templates

Large heart, page 157, and Large bird, page 159

1 Decide how many repeats of the heart and bird motif you would like. I spaced three at regular intervals along the sides and centred one at each end.

2 You'll find detailed instructions for iron-on appliqué on page 28. For each repeat you will need to trace two birds, two wings and a heart onto Bondaweb. Reverse one of the birds and its wing, so that they will face each other.

3 Fuse the wings and heart onto the floral print and iron one bird onto each of the ginghams. Varying the fabrics gives extra animation to the finished design, so mix and match the prints and checks for each pair of birds, their wings and the heart. I used three different ginghams in all: red, green and pink.

4 Fold the tablecloth into quarters and press the folds lightly to mark the centre of each side: use this crease as a guideline for ironing down the first motifs. You can then fold the long sides in half again, to mark the positions for the other two repeats.

5 Edge each individual piece, either with a round of short straight stitches or with a machine zigzag or satin stitch. Finish off by stitching the gingham ribbon around the edge of the cloth, mitring it at the corners and overlapping the ends with a neat hem.

top tip → IF YOUR SHEET HAS ANY INDELIBLE MARKS OR HOLES, YOU CAN CONCEAL THEM WITH CAREFULLY POSITIONED MOTIFS. WASH AND IRON THE APPLIQUE FABRICS FIRST, AS THE TABLECLOTH IS BOUND TO NEED LAUNDERING AT SOME STAGE AND ANY SHRINKAGE WILL DISTORT THE DESIGN.

Oven Glove

what you will need...

- 65 x 85cm cotton duck
- 45 x 80cm cotton batting
- 2.5m bias binding
- matching sewing thread
- sewing kit
- sewing machine

SKILL LEVEL

Here's another re-working of an everyday essential: even if you prefer heating up ready meals to baking wholemeal bread and trays of cupcakes, you'll need to have an oven glove! This project is very easy to put together and makes a good introduction to the techniques involved in binding edges.

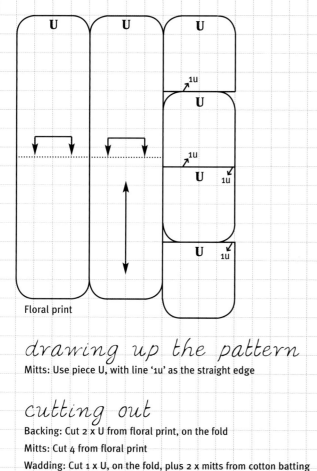

Floral print

drawing up the pattern

Mitts: Use piece U, with line '1u' as the straight edge

cutting out

Backing: Cut 2 x U from floral print, on the fold

Mitts: Cut 4 from floral print

Wadding: Cut 1 x U, on the fold, plus 2 x mitts from cotton batting

1 Start by stacking up the three pieces that make up the first mitt: a mitt with its right side down at the bottom, then a mitt padding in the middle and another mitt on top with its right side upwards.

2 Pin and tack all the layers together around the outside edge. Neaten the straight edge with bias binding, either by hand or machine, as shown in the steps on page 20. Do the same for the second mitt.

3 Sandwich the two backings and the remaining piece of padding together in the same way and tack close to the outside edge.

4 Pin a mitt at each end of the backing and tack in place. Sew a round of bias binding all the way round the outside edge, starting and finishing at the centre of one long edge.

5 Cut a 10cm length from the remaining binding and press under the ends. Fold in half widthways and slip stitch the folds together. Sew the ends securely to the point where the binding meets to make a hanging loop.

top tip

IF YOU'RE WORKING WITH A FABRIC THAT HAS A DIRECTIONAL DESIGN, LIKE THE STRIPES ON THIS 'FLORAL GINGHAM', PLAN THE POSITION OF THE PATTERN PIECES SO THAT THE DESIGN RUNS CENTRALLY ALONG THE BACKING AND MATCHES UP WITH THE MITTS AT EACH END. YOU MAY NEED EXTRA FABRIC FOR THIS.

Peg Bag

what you will need...

- 40 x 75cm cotton duck
- child-size coat hanger
- 1.5m bias binding
- matching sewing thread
- sewing kit
- sewing machine

SKILL LEVEL

Hanging out the washing is so much easier when your pegs are close to hand, as our grandmothers knew well. Here's another practical exercise in using bias binding: this time you can learn how to neaten inside curves, by stitching around the opening on this pretty and practical peg bag.

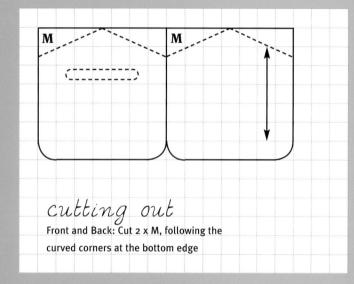

cutting out

Front and Back: Cut 2 x M, following the curved corners at the bottom edge

1 Lay the front face downwards and place the hanger centrally across the top, so that the base of the hook lines up with the edge. Draw along the top edge of the hanger, then cut along this line. Fold in half widthways to check the shape is symmetrical and trim as necessary.

2 Following the guideline on the cutting out diagram, draw in a narrow slit with rounded ends, 35cm up from the bottom edge. Work a line of reinforcing machine stitch 3mm outside the line. Using sharp embroidery scissors, cut out the centre to make the opening.

3 Neaten the opening with bias binding, sewn on by hand. So that the binding lies flat at the two ends you will need to pleat the centre and fan out the folded edges into a curve. Stitch the binding to the right side first, then the wrong side.

4 Pin the front to the back with wrong sides facing. Trim the top edge of the back so that it is the same shape as the front and tack the two pieces together.

5 Bind the outside edge of the peg bag, as shown on pages 20-21, starting at one side of the top point and remembering to leave a small gap for the hook. Insert the hanger through the opening and wriggle it about until the hook goes through the gap.

top tip →

IF YOU CAN'T FIND A 30CM COAT HANGER, YOU COULD TRY SHORTENING A STANDARD ONE. MEASURE UP AND MARK A CUTTING LINE 15CM FROM THE HOOK ON EACH ARM. CUT THE ENDS OFF CAREFULLY WITH A SMALL HACKSAW AND SMOOTH OFF ANY ROUGH EDGES WITH SANDPAPER.

Lavender Bags

SKILL LEVEL

Lavender has long been valued both for its fragrance and as a deterrent to moths. These hanging hearts and birds are filled with the dried buds, and will bring their gentle perfume to your wardrobe and linen cupboard. Sew them by hand or machine, for yourself or as presents for friends or family.

what you will need...

- 2 x 20cm squares of floral print cotton
- 35g dried lavender per bag
- 1 small button
- 15cm narrow tape
- paper and tracing paper
- matching sewing thread
- sewing kit
- sewing machine

templates

Large heart, page 157 and
Large bird, page 159

1 For the bird bag, trace off the body and wing outlines and cut them out. Pin the body template to the wrong side of the main fabric and draw around the edge. Cut out roughly, leaving about 1cm all round.

2 Cover the wing with the other fabric, following the turned edge appliqué method on page 29. Pin the wing to the right side of the bird making sure it lies in the correct position by holding the fabric up to the light. Slip stitch down.

3 With right sides facing, pin the front to the other fabric and machine stitch around the outline. Leave a 4cm gap along the straight edge at the back.

4 Trim the seam allowance back to 5mm all round, clipping and notching the curves as appropriate (see page 23). Press back the allowance on either side of the opening. Turn right side out, ease out the seams and press lightly.

5 Using a teaspoon, fill the bird with lavender, then slip stitch the opening.

6 Fold the tape in half to make a hanging loop and sew the ends to the bird's back, close to the top of the wing. Stitch on the button to make the eye.

7 The heart is made in the same way, with the opening along one straight edge, just above the point. Sew the hanging loop to the centre top.

top tip → SEWING CURVES ON A SMALL SCALE CAN BE FIDDLY, SO I CHEATED! INSTEAD OF CUTTING OUT THE FRONT AND BACK, THEN JOINING THE EDGES, SIMPLY DRAW THE MOTIF ONTO A PIECE OF FABRIC, TACK ANOTHER PIECE TO THE BACK, SEW TOGETHER AROUND THE OUTLINE AND TRIM THE SEAM.

Coat Hangers

SKILL LEVEL

Give your best frocks the special treatment they deserve, and prevent the shoulders from creasing, with these quick-to-make hangers. They have been padded in thrifty style by binding the wooden arms with old tights: you could also use strips cut from an old t-shirt or jumper.

what you will need...

- 20 x 65cm floral fabric
- wooden coat hanger
- padding: old tights or top cut into 10cm strips
- 60cm bias binding
- matching sewing thread
- sewing kit

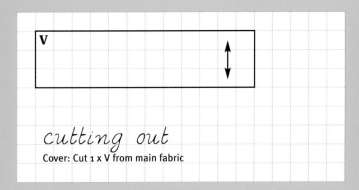

cutting out

Cover: Cut 1 x V from main fabric

1 Bind the padding around the coat hanger. Starting at one end, wrap it tightly towards, and then past, the hook. Sew on new lengths when needed and secure the ends with a few stitches.

2 Cut a length of binding 2cm longer than the hook. Press under a 5mm turning at one end. Fold in half lenthways and slip stitch the folded end and the long edges together to form a tube. Slide the open end over the hook and sew the raw ends to the padding.

3 Press a 1cm turning at the short edges and a 2cm turning along the long edges of the cover. Fold in half widthways and mark the centre point.

4 Slip stitch the folds at each short edge. Sew the top edges on the left side together, from the corner to the centre point. Use 5mm running stitches, worked 5mm down from the folds.

5 Slide the hanger into the cover. Pull up the thread so that the fabric gathers over the padding. Even out the folds and fasten off the thread. Gather the other side in the same way.

6 Make a bow from the remaining bias binding, trim the ends and stitch to the cover at the base of the hook.

top tip

A LENGTH OF DOUBLE-SIDED TAPE FIXED ALL THE WAY ACROSS THE ARMS OF THE HANGER WILL STOP THE PADDING FROM SLIPPING ABOUT AS YOU WIND IT IN PLACE.

Lavender Pillow

what you will need...

- 35 x 85cm floral fabric
- 300g dried lavender
- 1.8m 5cm-wide lace
- 8 x 1cm buttons
- matching sewing thread
- sewing kit
- sewing machine

SKILL LEVEL

Keep this scented pillow on your bed and the soothing qualities of lavender will always bring you the sweetest dreams. To keep the contents evenly distributed and to give it an upholstered look, the front and back have been stitched together at four central points and trimmed with mother of pearl buttons.

cutting out

Front and Back: Cut 2 x N

1 Mark the four button positions on both pieces, as shown on the diagram. With right sides facing, pin the two together. Machine stitch, with a 1cm seam allowance, leaving a 10cm gap in the centre of one edge.

2 Press the seam allowance back on either side of the gap. Clip the corners and turn right side out. Ease the corners into shape and press the seams.

3 Fill the bag with lavender by pouring it through a funnel made from a rolled-up sheet of paper. Slip stitch the gap to close.

4 Sew a button onto a cross at the front, then pass the needle right through to the back, so that it comes out at the corresponding mark. Add another button and stitch the two together through the pillow several times. Do the same at the other three crosses.

5 Pin the lace along one side edge of the pillow. Measure and mark off the next 10cm, then pin along the top so that the spare lace forms a loop at the corner. Pin the lace to the other two edges and join the ends.

6 Slip stitch the lace to the seams. Sew a line of running stitches along the straight edge of each loop as you reach it and pull up the thread to gather the lace. Slip stitch the gathers securely to the corner.

top tip → YOU CAN INTERPRET THIS PROJECT IN SEVERAL WAYS, BY VARYING THE SIZE AND SHAPE (A SQUARE OR LARGE HEART PERHAPS) OR BY CUTTING THE FRONT AND BACK FROM DIFFERENT FABRICS AND USING DIFFERENT TYPES OF BUTTONS ON EACH SIDE TO MAKE THE PILLOW REVERSIBLE.

Quilted Hottie

SKILL LEVEL

This hand-quilted hot water bottle cover, made from pink paisley fabric, was inspired by traditional feather eiderdowns. It is trimmed with a pale turquoise print and fastens with a rouleau loop and a pearl button. Snuggle up close and your hottie will keep you warm and snug on the coldest winter night.

what you will need...

- 50 x 60cm paisley fabric
- 50 x 60cm polyester or cotton batting
- 50 x 60cm backing fabric
- 15 x 40cm binding fabric
- matching sewing thread
- 50cm narrow velvet ribbon
- 1 x 12mm button
- sewing kit
- sewing machine

Paisley fabric

Contrast fabric

drawing up the pattern

Top Front: Use piece W, with line 1w as the bottom edge

Main Front: Use piece W, with line 2w as the top edge

Back: Use piece W, tracing around the entire outline

cutting out

Top Front: Cut 1 from paisley fabric

Main Front: Cut 1 from paisley fabric

Back: Cut 1 from paisley fabric

Binding: Cut 2 x L from contrast fabric

Button Loop: Cut 1 x X from contrast fabric, on the bias

top tip THE PATTERN DIAGRAM IS FOR A STANDARD SHAPE, BUT CHECK THAT YOUR OWN HOTTIE LIES COMFORTABLY WITHIN THE MARKED SEAM LINE, WITH AT LEAST 2CM EXTRA ALL ROUND. INCREASE THE LENGTH OR WIDTH IF NECESSARY FOR A PERFECT FIT.

Quilted Hottie

1 You will find all you need to know about hand quilting in the techniques section, so refer back to page 29 for the next two steps. Start by marking a 3mm diamond grid on the right side of each of the three cover pieces.

2 Cut out a piece of batting and a piece of backing fabric, each of which is slightly larger all round than the main front panel. Tack the three layers together, quilt along the lines and around the outside edges, then trim. Make up the other top front and back in the same way.

3 Bind the straight edges of the two front panels with the contrast strips, as shown on page 20.

4 See page 25 for how to make a rouleau buttonhole from the bias strip. Trim it down to 6cm and fold in half to form a loop. Sew the ends securely to the wrong side of the top front panel, half way along the straight edge.

5 Place the back panel, right side up, on your work surface. Lay the top front panel, face down, across the top so the curved edges are lined up exactly. Position the front panel over them both so that the bottom and side edges match.

6 Pin the three pieces together around the outside edge.

Tack and machine stitch, leaving a 1cm seam allowance. Clip and notch the curves (see page 23), then turn right side out and ease the curves into shape.

7 Cut the ribbon in half and tie each piece in a little bow. Cut off the ends at a sharp angle and sew one to each side of the neck. Sew the button to the centre of the front panel, just below the loop.

top tip → THIS PROJECT IS AN EXCELLENT WAY TO LEARN HOW TO HAND QUILT, BUT IF YOU DON'T FANCY ALL THAT EXTRA STITCHING YOU COULD SIMPLY CUT THE BATTING AND BACKING TO THE SAME SIZE AS THE THREE COVER PIECES AND MAKE A PLAIN BUT PADDED COVER!

Bath Hat

what you will need...

- 60cm square of floral print
- 60cm square of waterproof fabric
- 2m bias binding
- 2m narrow lace
- 1m hat elastic
- 2 small safety pins
- matching sewing thread
- sewing kit
- sewing machine

SKILL LEVEL

This flowery bath hat is so pretty that you won't ever want to put it away in your bathroom cupboard. It is very easy to make, from a surprisingly large gathered circle of cotton duck or lighter weight cotton, which is lined with waterproof fabric and trimmed with a frill of broderie anglaise.

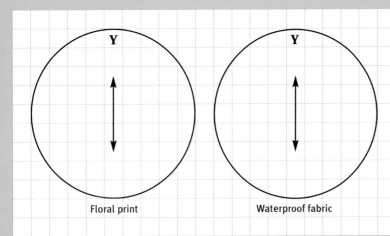

Floral print

Waterproof fabric

cutting out

Hat: Cut 1 x Y from floral print

Lining: Cut 1 x Y from waterproof fabric

1 Pin the lining to the wrong side of the hat and tack them both together all the way around the circumference.

2 Open out one fold of the bias binding and turn under 1cm at the end. With right sides together, tack the binding all around the circumference so that the unfolded raw edge lies along the outside edge of the hat. You'll find details of how to do this on page 21.

3 Trim the other end of the binding to 1cm when you've got all the way round and turn it under so that the two ends butt closely together. Trim the seam allowance back to 3mm.

4 Turn the folded edge of the binding to the wrong side and slip stitch the fold along the curved seam line.

5 Sew the straight edge of the lace to the right side of the hat along the bottom edge of the binding, with the scalloped edge facing outwards. Trim and seam the two ends.

6 Tie the elastic securely to a safety pin. Use another pin to fasten the loose end of the elastic close to the gap in the binding, so that it won't disappear as you gather up the hat.

7 Thread the elastic through the gap and around the binding, pulling it up as you go. Check that you have a comfortable fit, then knot and stitch the ends together. Trim to 2cm and slide the knot so that it is hidden within the binding.

top tip → I USED A WOVEN SHOWER CURTAIN MATERIAL TO MAKE THE WATERPROOF (BUT NOT WATER-TIGHT!) LINING FOR THE HAT. THIS IS SOFTER AND MORE COMFORTABLE TO WEAR THAN OTHER FABRICS WITH A PLASTICISED FINISH.

Needlecase & Pincushion

SKILL LEVEL

If you've got the sewing bug, you'll need plenty of different needles for plain stitching, embroidery and quilting. Store them safely in the pages of this handy book, then make the adorable pincushion to match. Don't put your needles in the cushion however – they may disappear into the filling!

what you will need...

- 40 x 35cm floral print cotton duck
- 30cm square felt
- bondaweb
- thin card
- pinking shears
- press stud
- 25cm narrow ribbon
- polyester toy filling
- matching sewing thread
- sewing kit
- sewing machine

template

Small heart, page 157

Z | **Floral print** 4Z | 1Z 2Z 3Z
Thin card | | Felt

cutting out

Needlecase cover: Cut 1 x Z from thin card and 1 x Z from floral print cotton duck, adding approximately 1cm all round

Needlecase pages: Cut 1 x 1Z, 1 x 2Z and 1 x 3Z from felt, using pinking shears

Tab: Cut 2 x 4Z from floral print cotton duck

1 To make the pincushion, trace round the heart template onto the wrong side of the floral fabric. Cut out roughly, 1cm from the line. Cut another piece of fabric the same size and tack the two together with right sides facing.

2 Machine stitch around the outline, leaving a 4cm gap in one straight side. Trim the allowance to 6mm, then clip and notch it as shown on page 23. Press the allowance back on both sides of the gap and turn right side out.

3 Stuff the pincushion with your chosen filling, packing it down firmly through the gap. Close the gap with slip stitch.

4 Tie the velvet ribbon into a small bow and trim the ends into fishtails. Sew the bow to the centre top of the finished heart pincushion.

ALTERNATIVE PINCUSHION FILLINGS OVER THE YEARS HAVE INCLUDED SAWDUST; CLEAN SHEEP'S FLEECE WHICH CONTAINS NATURAL LANOLIN; COFFEE GROUNDS TO PREVENT RUST, AND SAND OR EMERY POWDER WHICH GIVE YOU A HEAVIER CUSHION AND KEEP THE POINTS SHARP.

Needlecase
& Pincushion

1 To make the needlecase, cut a rectangle of Bondaweb 1cm larger on each side than the card cover. Iron this to the floral fabric and cut out around the edge. Peel off the backing paper.

2 Place the fabric on your ironing board with the Bondaweb facing upwards, then position the card centrally on top.

3 Fold the corners of the fabric over the card, gently pressing them down in turn with the tip of your iron. Now fold the sides over and iron each one so that the corners are neatly mitred.

4 Turn the cover the other way up and, protecting the surface with a piece of spare fabric, iron it gently so the fabric fuses onto the card. Stitch the recessed half of the press stud halfway down the right side, 2cm in from the edge.

5 Stitch the other half of the press stud to the round end of one tab, on the right side. Tack and machine stitch the two tabs together around the long and curved edges, leaving a 5mm seam allowance. Notch the allowance around the curve and turn right side out.

6 Trace the cover lining (1Z) onto the paper side of the Bondaweb. Cut out roughly, then iron it onto the felt. Cut along the pencil line with pinking shears.

7 Pin the other two pages centrally on top and machine stitch together down the centre. Peel off the backing paper from the first page, then press it onto the cover.

top tip →

BUY SEVERAL PACKETS OF NEEDLES IN VARIOUS SHAPES AND SIZES AND TRANSFER THEM TO YOUR COMPLETED NEEDLECASE, KEEPING ONE TYPE ON EACH FELT PAGE. YOU'LL ALSO FIND IT USEFUL TO ADD A FEW ASSORTED SAFETY PINS AND PERHAPS A NEEDLE THREADER.

Knitting Bag

what you will need...

- selection of dress weight cotton fabrics
- old envelopes and paper
- 55 x 125cm floral print
- 2 round bag handles
- matching sewing thread
- sewing kit
- sewing machine

template
Hexagon, page 156

SKILL LEVEL

Hexagon patchwork, with its characteristic honeycomb pattern, was hugely popular in Victorian times and once again in the Seventies, when it was used to create countless bedcovers and cushions. It's time for another revival of this absorbing hand technique: start off with this useful knitting bag.

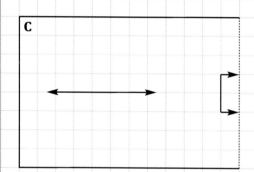

Floral print

cutting out
Lining: Cut 1 x C from floral print, on the fold

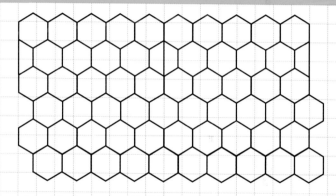

Layout for Hexagons and Half hexagons

1 Make 60 paper hexagons using the template as a guide, and cut two of them in half, from point to point.

2 Cut out a piece of fabric 1cm larger all round than the hexagon. Don't worry about being too accurate – just make sure it is big enough to cover the template comfortably.

3 Pin a hexagon centrally to the wrong side of the fabric. Turning down one edge at a time and making a neat fold at each angle, tack the surplus fabric to the paper.

top tip → IF YOU WANT YOUR DESIGN TO HAVE AN OVERALL THEME, KEEP TO A LIMITED COLOUR PALETTE, AS I DID. FOR A MORE RANDOM, HAPHAZARD LOOK, JUST GO FOR ALL THE FABRICS YOU CAN FIND: TAKE A LOOK AT THE FABULOUS VINTAGE BEDSPREAD ON PAGES 86–87 TO SEE WHAT I MEAN!

Knitting Bag

4 Join the first two patches by lining them up with right sides facing, and slip stitching through two adjacent edges. Make small, closely spaced stitches and pass the needle through the fabric only, not the papers. Sew two sides of the third hexagon into the angle between the first two.

5 Continue building up all 62 patches into a mosaic, following the layout diagram. Stitch the first 40 together in four staggered rows of ten.

6 Sew half-hexagons at the ends of the fifth row and, working inwards, add four more hexagons to each side and two more half-hexagons in the centre, but don't join these two patches together.

7 For the sixth row, sew five hexagons at each end without joining the two in the centre.

8 Press the finished patchwork and fold it in half with right sides facing. Join the edges of the hexagons at the ends of the bottom three rows, to make the bag.

9 Unpick all the papers (you can reuse these for another project). Trim a shallow triangle from the edge of each hexagon on the top and bottom rows to make straight edges, taking care not to cut into the seams.

10 Fold the bag, wrong side out, so that the openings lie at the side edges. Pin the front and back together along the bottom edge and machine stitch, leaving a 1cm seam allowance. Turn the right side out.

11 Fold the lining in half lengthways, with right sides facing, and pin the side edges together. Make a 25cm seam, from the corner upwards on each side, 5cm from the edge. Trim 10cm from the top edge. Press down the remaining seam allowances at the sides, then press under 1cm along the top edges.

12 Slip the lining inside the bag. Pin and slip stitch the folded side edges to the patchwork. Machine stitch the top edge of the patchwork to the lining at the front and back, where they meet.

13 Fold the top edge of the front lining over to the bag, passing it through the first handle. Pin the folded edge to the patchwork as you go, just below the line of machine stitching. Slip stitch in place, then repeat at the back.

top tip

PATCHWORK ORIGINATED AT A TIME WHEN NEW MATERIALS WERE EXPENSIVE AND OFTEN HARD TO COME BY. MAINTAIN THE TRADITION — AND YOUR GREEN CREDENTIALS — BY SAVING ALL YOUR OFFCUTS, ALONG WITH YOUR FAMILY'S OLD GARMENTS, TO MAKE YOUR HEXAGONS.

Knitting Needle Case

- 45 x 50cm floral print
- 45 x 55cm spotted fabric
- 45cm nylon zip
- 75cm bias binding
- matching sewing thread
- sewing kit
- sewing machine

SKILL LEVEL

Don't be put off by the idea of sewing in a zip – it's not nearly as complicated as you might think! I chose a bright red one for this long thin knitting needle case, which echoes the colour of the roses and stands out well against the spotty lining.

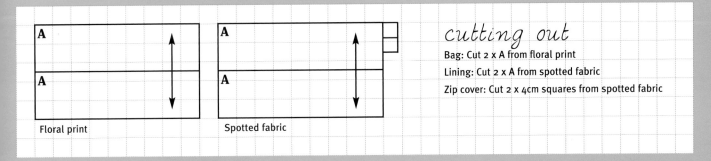

Floral print   Spotted fabric

cutting out

Bag: Cut 2 x A from floral print

Lining: Cut 2 x A from spotted fabric

Zip cover: Cut 2 x 4cm squares from spotted fabric

1 With right sides facing, pin and machine stitch one long edge of a lining piece to a bag piece, with a 5mm allowance. Press the seam away from the lining.

2 Fold along the seam line with wrong sides together, and press so that 5mm of the lining is visible above the top edge of the bag. Trim the bottom edge of the front so that it is the same depth as the lining. Join the other two pieces in the same way.

3 Fold the two small squares in half. Tack one across each end of the closed zip, with the folds facing inwards. Double check the length against the bag and adjust if necessary.

4 Open the zip. Tack one side of the bag to one side of the zip so that the teeth lie just below the top edge. Do the same on the other side and close the zip.

5 Fit a zip foot and, from the right side, machine stitch the zip to the bag, 3mm below the seam line. Sew across the zip at each end, 1cm from the edge.

6 Fold the bag with right sides facing, so that the zip lies in the middle. Tack the side and bottom edges together, then machine stitch leaving a 1cm seam. Trim the allowance to 4mm and bind to neaten (see page 20). Turn right side out.

top tip

THE FINISHED SIZE OF 43CM MEANS THAT THIS BAG IS LONG ENOUGH FOR MOST STANDARD KNITTING NEEDLES, BUT IF YOU HAVE GOT SOME EXTRA BIG PAIRS AMONGST YOUR COLLECTION, INCREASE THE LENGTH ACCORDINGLY SO THAT THEY WILL FIT IN.

Girl's Apron

what you will need...

- 50cm square cotton duck
- 40 x 85cm spotted cotton duck
- matching sewing thread
- sewing kit
- sewing machine

templates

Large heart, page 157

SKILL LEVEL

It's not always easy to keep children clean when they're in the kitchen, but here are two aprons that may help! The girl's version has contrasting bound edges whilst the boy's one overleaf is quicker to make and a perfect beginner's project. Swap the fabrics as you wish, to suit your sewing skills – and your child.

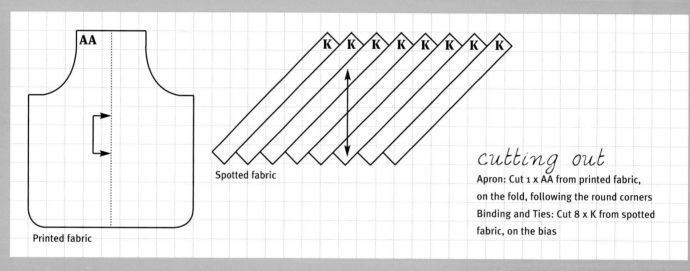

AA

Spotted fabric

Printed fabric

cutting out

Apron: Cut 1 x AA from printed fabric, on the fold, following the round corners
Binding and Ties: Cut 8 x K from spotted fabric, on the bias

1 You'll find all you need to know about bias binding on pages 20-21. Following the steps, join the spotted strips, then use them to bind around the neck and the lower half of the apron. Top stitch 3mm from the edge.

2 Mark a point 25cm away from the centre of the remaining binding. This gives you the size of the neck loop, which you can adjust as necessary.

3 Open out one fold of the binding and pin the first mark to the left edge of the neck, with raw edges together. Pin and

sew the binding to the apron, following the instructions for inside curves. Do the same at the other side.

4 Tack the two folded edges of the binding together around the neck loop.

5 Trim the ties to the same length, and press under 1cm at each end. Tack the folded edges together. Starting at the end of one tie, and finishing at the other, top stitch all the way along the binding, 3mm from the edge.

6 Make the pocket from the remaining spotted fabric, as for steps 1 and 2 of the pincushion on page 77. Slip stitch the gap, press and top stitch around the edge. Pin the pocket to the apron and sew down along the straight edges.

top tip

GIVE YOUR APRON A CO-ORDINATED LOOK BY PICKING OUT A COLOUR FROM THE MAIN FABRIC TO USE FOR THE POCKET AND BINDING. I MATCHED THE BLUE POLKA DOT FABRIC TO THE STRAWBERRY FLOWERS, AND AS A BONUS, THE SPOTS ECHO THE SEED PATTERN ON THE RED FRUIT.

Boy's Apron

what you will need...

- 60 x 50cm dressweight print fabric
- 60 x 50cm white cotton
- 45 x 50cm red cotton
- bondaweb
- stranded embroidery thread in matching colours
- 2 D-rings
- matching sewing thread
- sewing kit
- sewing machine

SKILL LEVEL

Make this apron for the junior cowboy of the family, as even tough guys have to stay tidy sometimes. Curved seams, like those on either side of the bib, can be a bit tricky if you have to hem or bind them, but this apron's made in a special cheat's way which avoids any complicated techniques. Yee hah!

Print fabric

White cotton

Red cotton

BB

cutting out

Apron: Cut 1 x AA from print fabric, on the fold, following square corners

Backing: Cut 1 x AA from white cotton, on the fold, following square corners

Neck Loop and Ties: Cut 3 x L from red cotton, on the fold

Pocket: Cut 1 x BB from red cotton, on the fold

1 Pin the front to the lining around the side and bottom edges, with right sides facing. Seam together, 1cm from the edge, leaving the neck open. Clip the corners, notch the curves (see pages 22–23). Turn right side out. Press under the seam allowance at the neck and slip stitch the edges together.

2 Make a 1cm double seam along the top of the pocket and top stitch both edges. This will lie at the front. Press under a 1cm seam at the other sides, so that the fabric is turned to the back.

3 Press the pocket in half lengthways to mark the centre. Cut a few motifs from the offcuts and appliqué them with Bondaweb (see page 28). Edge each shape with straight stitches. Embroider the lassoes in chain stitch and the grass with straight stitches.

4 Sew the pocket in place and add a line of stitching down the centre.

5 Make two red strips into ties, as on page 27, neatening them at both ends. Sew one to each side of the apron with decorative reinforcing stitching.

6 Cut 10cm from the third strip, and make a tie from each piece. Slip the short length through the two D-rings. Fold in half and stitch the ends to the left corner of the neck edge as before. Sew the other tie to the right corner and loop the end through the rings.

top tip

THE COMIC STRIP COWBOYS ARE GREAT FUN TO DO AND TO WEAR. IF YOU ARE MAKING A MORE GIRLY APRON YOU COULD MAKE A SIMILAR POCKET WITH LEAVES AND BLOOMS CUT FROM FLOWERED FABRIC, OR USE ONE OF THE MOTIFS AT THE BACK OF THE BOOK FOR A SIMPLER DESIGN.

Stanley Picture

SKILL LEVEL

Stanley, my Lakeland Terrier, has become something of a design icon in his own right. He even has a special fabric to himself, called 'Mini Stanley'. This iron-on appliqué picture is based on one of the motifs in that print and shows him proudly sporting his best vintage floral coat and a spotty collar.

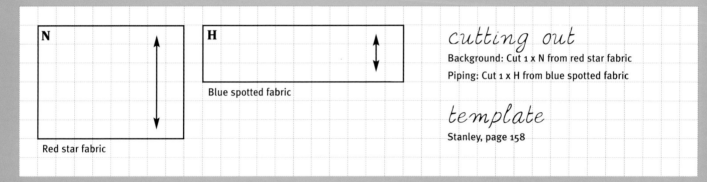

what you will need...

- bondaweb
- 35 x 45cm red star fabric
- 20 x 80cm blue spotted fabric
- scraps of floral and green fabric
- small button
- matching sewing thread
- 1m piping cord
- 18 x 26cm block of wood, padded with wadding on one side
- hammer and tacks or staplegun
- sewing kit

N ↕
Red star fabric

H ↕
Blue spotted fabric

cutting out
Background: Cut 1 x N from red star fabric
Piping: Cut 1 x H from blue spotted fabric

template
Stanley, page 158

1 Trace the main Stanley outline onto Bondaweb, reversing the image if you wish him to face to the right. Following the steps on page 28, cut him out from blue spotted fabric, and iron him centrally onto the red fabric.

2 Add a matching ear, then make his collar from green spotted fabric and his coat from the floral print. Sew on the button for his eye.

3 Place the finished appliqué face downwards and position the wooden block on top, making sure that it lies centrally over Stanley. Turn back the top edge and tack or staple it onto the wood. Now turn back the opposite edge, stretching it slightly and fix that down too. Secure the side edges in the same way.

4 To make the piping, press the strip of spotted fabric in half lengthways and cut along the fold. Sew the two pieces together and press the seam open, then cover the cord as shown on page 23.

5 Tack the cord around the edge of the covered block, joining the round as shown, and staple or tack the loose fabric to the back.

top tip

LOOK OUT FOR A CHARACTERFUL OLD CARVED FRAME AS AN ALTERNATIVE WAY TO DISPLAY YOUR PICTURE: IT DOESN'T MATTER IF THE GLASS IS MISSING OR IF THERE ARE A FEW KNOCKS AND CHIPS AS YOU CAN EASILY REVIVE THE WOODWORK WITH A COAT OR TWO OF PAINT.

Bird Mobile

what you will need...

- 45cm square mini print fabric
- scraps of other fabrics
- polyester toy filling
- black 3mm rocaille beads
- strong white beading thread
- 2 25cm garden sticks
- curtain ring or split ring
- matching sewing thread
- sewing kit
- sewing machine

SKILL LEVEL

Mix and match your leftover scraps of fabric to make these little bobbing birds, switching them around on wings and bodies. A jumble of mini prints always works well, so I chose three favourites, featuring roses, buds and stars, then added a paisley and a vintage rose print in the same colour palette.

cutting out

Binding: Cut 1 x K from floral print, on the bias

Cut the strip in half lengthways

template

Small bird, page 159

1 Trace the bird's body and wing outlines onto paper and cut out. Draw round the body template onto the wrong side of a piece of fabric. Cut out roughly and, with right sides facing, pin to a second piece of the same fabric. Tack close to the outline.

2 Stitch around the outline, leaving a 3cm gap along the back. The lavender bird diagram on page 65 will show you how to do this.

3 Cut out, leaving a 6mm seam allowance. Press back the allowance along the opening, then clip and notch the curves. Turn right side out, stuff gently with toy filling and close the gap with slip stitch. Sew a bead to each side of the head for the eyes.

4 Make two wings in the same way. Turn right side out, press and slip stitch to the finished bird.

GIVE EACH OF YOUR FLOCK ITS OWN INDIVIDUAL CHARACTER BY VARYING THE POSITION OF THE HANGING THREADS, AND THE ANGLE AT WHICH YOU SEW THE WINGS.

Bird
Mobile

5 Bind each stick with a bias strip, wrapping it diagonally, and stitching down the ends. Hold them together in a cross, and bind the centre with thread or a very narrow strip of fabric. A few stitches, worked through the bindings, will keep the sticks securely fixed.

6 Stitch a 30cm length of beading thread to the end of each arm of the cross and knot the loose ends together. Tie the ends to the ring and trim.

7 Sew a length of beading thread to the back of each bird. Stitch the loose ends to the centre and tips of the cross. Hang each one of them at a different length, making sure the centre bird has the longest thread.

top tip → THE BIRDS ARE GOING TO APPEAL TO EVERYBODY WHO SEES THEM, BUT FOR SAFETY'S SAKE, PLEASE KEEP THE MOBILE WELL OUT OF THE REACH OF THE SMALLEST MEMBERS OF YOUR FAMILY.

Stanley Toy

SKILL LEVEL

Lucky mascot Stanley is one of the smallest projects in the book, but – as you may expect – I have to admit that it is my favourite! He's stitched completely by hand, and can be made in an afternoon. This pet print was just the right fabric to use, but you could vary the look with spots on both sides or a mini floral design.

1 Cut out a paper Stanley template. Pin to the wrong side of the printed fabric so that his nose is pointing left. Trim the seam to 5mm, then notch and clip as on page 23. Fold the seam allowance over and tack it to the paper. Press and remove the paper.

2 Make the back in the same way, with Stanley facing to the right. Slip stitch the ricrac around the edge, so that the scallops project beyond the fold.

3 Pin the front to the back, sandwiching the ricrac between the two. Slip stitch together, leaving a gap along Stanley's tummy. Stuff the body with your chosen filling, a spoonful at a time, then close the gap.

4 Cut out the ear template and make two shapes from printed fabric as for the body. Slip stitch them together and sew in place along the top edge only. Add a narrow strip of felt for the collar.

5 To make his nametag, write 'Stan' on the red felt and work tiny back stitches over the letters. Cut out, using a coin to give you a neat circle, and sew the tag to the collar. Finish off with a tiny button for Stanley's eye.

what you will need...

- 20cm square printed fabric
- 20cm blue spotted fabric
- 1m red ricrac
- tiny button
- scraps of red and green felt
- green embroidery thread
- filling
- sewing kit

template
Stanley, page 156

top tip BEAN BAGS ARE USUALLY STUFFED WITH LENTILS OR RICE, TO GIVE THEIR CHARACTERISTIC WEIGHT AND TEXTURE. SUCH FILLINGS, HOWEVER, WON'T STAND UP TO THE DAMP SO YOU COULD USE THE NEWER ALTERNATIVE – SPECIALLY MADE NYLON BEADS FROM GOOD CRAFT SUPPLIERS.

Cot Quilt

templates

Elephant, page 155 and
Small bird, page 157

SKILL LEVEL

Here are the birds again, this time sitting alongside their
elephant friends on a charming cot quilt. The time and skill
involved in stitching patchwork makes it a true labour of love,
so this would be a wonderful present for a newborn. The pink
and blue colour scheme makes it suitable for a girl or boy.

what you will need...

- 65 x 140cm floral print
- 45 x 140cm pink spotted fabric
- 55 x 140cm blue spotted fabric
- 80 x 120cm cotton batting
- 80 x 120cm backing fabric
- sewing kit
- sewing machine
- twin needle for machine (optional)

Floral print

Pink spotted fabric

Blue spotted fabric

drawing up the pattern

Top and Bottom Borders: Using A as a
width guide, cut 2 x 12.5 x 105cm strips
Side Borders: Using A as a width guide,
cut 2 x 65cm strips

cutting out

Elephant Blocks: Cut 8 x CC from floral print
Bird Blocks: Cut 7 x DD from floral print
and 28 EE from pink spotted fabric
Corner Squares: Cut 4 x BB from pink spotted fabric
Top and Bottom Borders: Cut 2 from blue spotted fabric
Side Borders: Cut 2 from blue spot

top tip

DEPENDING ON YOUR SKILL AND PATIENCE YOU CAN OMIT THE
TWIN STITCHING AND CROSS STITCHES, AND INSTEAD HAND QUILT
THE ENTIRE SURFACE OF THE PATCHWORK, OUTLINING EACH OF THE
BLOCKS, AND IF YOU'VE TIME, THE ELEPHANTS AND THE BIRDS.

Cot Quilt

The seam allowance throughout is 1cm

1 Referring to page 28, cut out eight Bondaweb elephants from blue spotted fabric, four facing right and four left. Iron them centrally on to the large squares. Add blue tails and pink ears and eyes. Straight stitch around each shape, with matching thread. Embroider the eyes with black cross stitches.

2 Fix a blue bird to each of the small squares, three facing right and four of them facing to the left. Give each one a pink wing and an embroidered eye. Sew a pink triangle to each side of the square and press the seams inwards.

3 With right sides facing, pin the blocks together in five rows of three: three rows with the elephants on the outside, facing inwards, and two rows with the birds at the outside, also looking at each other. Machine stitch together.

4 Press all the seams towards the elephant blocks, then join the five rows together matching the seams exactly. Fit the twin needle to your sewing machine and work a line of double stitching over each long seam.

5 Sew the side borders to the quilt and press the seams open. Sew the remaining four spotted squares to each end of the top and bottom borders. Press the seams open, then pin and stitch in place, matching the seams at the corner squares.

6 Press the seams open and machine stitch along the top and bottom edges of the patchwork, as before. Press a 1cm turning along each outside edge.

7 Lay the quilt out flat with the right side facing downwards. Place the batting centrally across it, with the backing fabric on top. Pin the three layers together. Turn over and work a cross stitch across the corners of each block to secure the layers.

8 Finish off by turning the surplus fabric to the back, folding the corners over neatly. Pin down and slip stitch the fold to the backing.

ANYTHING THAT COMES INTO CONTACT WITH BABIES AND SMALL CHILDREN WILL UNDOUBTEDLY NEED TO BE LAUNDERED AT REGULAR INTERVALS, SO DON'T FORGET TO WASH AND PRESS YOUR FABRIC BEFORE YOU START TO AVOID ANY SHRINKAGE OR COLOUR RUNS AT A LATER DATE.

Heart Quilt

SKILL LEVEL

Making an appliqué quilt on the scale of this stunning hearts and flowers design, has always been a major undertaking, but contemporary techniques mean that it will take much less time than you may expect! You will find detailed step-by-step instructions for iron-on appliqué on page 28.

what you will need...

- 145 x 140cm white cotton
- 65 x 125cm floral print fabric for the border
- 75 x 140cm each of three different print fabrics
- 150 x 180cm print fabric for the backing (join as necessary)
- 150 x 180cm cotton batting
- 3m x 44cm-wide bondaweb
- quilter's safety pins (optional)
- quilting thread
- matching sewing thread
- sewing kit
- sewing machine

M	M	M	M	M
M	M	M	M	M

Q	
Q	
Q	
Q	
Q	Cut 3

Floral print

cutting out

Flower Blocks: Cut 10 x M from white cotton following square corners

Heart Blocks: Cut 10 x M from three different print fabrics following square corners

Border Strips: Cut 3 x Q and 4 x Q, on the fold, from one print fabric

templates

Large Heart, page 157 and
Large Flower, page 160

top tip → THE FINISHED QUILT MEASURES 142 x 175CM – THE PERFECT SIZE TO GO OVER A STANDARD SINGLE BED. ADD ONE OR MORE ROWS OF SQUARES TO THE SIDE EDGE IF YOU NEED TO MAKE IT WIDE ENOUGH FOR A QUEEN, DOUBLE OR A EVEN KING-SIZED BED.

Heart Quilt

1 To make a flower block, cut a flower, two leaves and a stalk, each from a different print. Iron onto a white square. Select a new combination for each of the ten blocks. Edge the shapes with straight stitch, worked in matching thread.

2 Appliqué four matching hearts to each of the printed squares, positioning them centrally, with points facing inwards. Mix and match the prints so that all ten blocks look different.

3 Alternating hearts and flowers, arrange the completed blocks in five rows of four, in a chequerboard pattern.

4 Join the horizontal rows, leaving a 1cm seam allowance. Press all the seams open. Pin the top two rows together, matching the seams exactly, then stitch 1cm from the edge. Press seams open. Join the other three rows in the same way.

5 Spread out the backing, face downwards. Lay the wadding on top, then place the quilt top centrally over the two. Starting from the centre, pin or tack all three layers together. Firstly work out towards the four corners, then to the midpoint of each side.

6 Now work a row of tacking or pin a line along the centre of each row of blocks, so that you end up with a grid pattern across the surface, with a cross joining the corners. Finish by sewing or pinning all around the outside edge of the quilt top.

7 Using quilting thread and a short needle, stitch along each seam line: quilters call this 'stitching in the ditch'. If you prefer to sew by machine use a 'walking foot' to prevent puckering. Trim the backing and batting to 5cm all round.

8 Leaving a 1cm allowance, join all the border strips and press the seams open. Cut two 170cm lengths from this strip and press under a 1cm turning along one long edge of each.

9 With right sides facing and raw edges together, pin and stitch the 170cm side border strips to the side edges of the patchwork, leaving 2cm overlapping the border at each end. Press outwards. Add two 145cm top and bottom border strips in the same way.

10 Pin the overlapping border to the back of the quilt and slip stitch in place along the folded edges.

I CHOSE ALL THREE DIFFERENT VERSIONS OF MY VINTAGE-INSPIRED 'ROSE PAISLEY' PRINT TO MAKE THIS QUILT. THIS UNEXPECTED COMBINATION GIVES A UNIQUE AND SUBTLE APPEARANCE TO THE HEART BLOCKS, WHERE THE COLOURS BLEND HARMONIOUSLY.

Aeroplane Blanket

SKILL LEVEL

Working with felt appeals to children and adults alike because it is so quick and easy to use. It comes in bright primary colours and has the advantage of not fraying, even when cut into intricate shapes. This cosy blanket is a great project to make together, as a way to learn about appliqué and stitching.

1 Turn up and tack down a 1cm double hem all around the outside edge of the fleece square.

2 Using a large crewel needle threaded with tapestry yarn, work a round of blanket stitch to keep the hem in place.

3 Following the detailed steps for iron-on appliqué on page 28, trace off the various parts of the aeroplanes onto Bondaweb, reversing one of the motifs. You can follow the colours I used or make up your own variation.

4 Lightly iron down the bodies of the aircraft first, using a pressing cloth to protect the surface of the felt and fleece. Add the windows, wings and tails.

5 Finish off by stitching around each individual shape with small straight stitches in thread to match each of the different colours of felt.

top tip

I APPLIQUED THIS TRIO OF JET LINERS ONTO A BACKGROUND OF SOFT FLEECE, BUT THEY WOULD ALSO CHEER UP AN OLD WOOLLEN BLANKET OR PLAIN BEDCOVER. IF YOU HAVE AN AVIATION ENTHUSIAST IN THE FAMILY, YOU COULD ADD A WHOLE FLEET TO A SET OF MATCHING CUSHIONS.

Beanie Cushion

SKILL LEVEL

Squashy bean bags are fun to have in bedrooms or playrooms. This one has a toddler-sized handle, so its young owner can drag it from place to place, then nestle down. The cover is bound to get grubby, so I inserted a zip for easy removal.

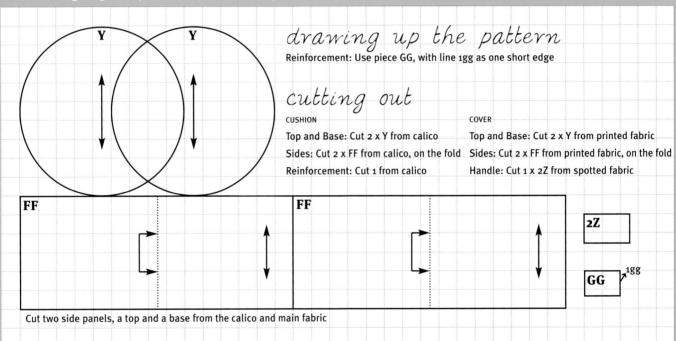

drawing up the pattern

Reinforcement: Use piece GG, with line 1gg as one short edge

cutting out

CUSHION

Top and Base: Cut 2 x Y from calico

Sides: Cut 2 x FF from calico, on the fold

Reinforcement: Cut 1 from calico

COVER

Top and Base: Cut 2 x Y from printed fabric

Sides: Cut 2 x FF from printed fabric, on the fold

Handle: Cut 1 x 2Z from spotted fabric

Cut two side panels, a top and a base from the calico and main fabric

The seam allowance throughout is 1.5cm

1 Join the short edges of the calico sides, leaving a 20cm gap in one seam. Press the seams open and press back the unstitched allowance. Add the top and base, as shown on page 23. Turn right side out, fill with beads and join the gap.

2 Make up the handle as on page 27, then join the ends and press the seam open. Pin to the centre of the cover top, on the right side. Pin the reinforcement to the wrong side, directly behind the handle. Machine stitch the handle in place.

3 Press under 3cm along one left and one right edge of the side panels. Sew the zip between these edges (see page 25) and slip stitch the folds together for 2.5cm at each end.

4 Open the zip and add top and base as before. Turn right sides out and press lightly. Insert the cushion and do up zip.

top tip

GETTING THE FILLED CUSHION INSIDE THE COVER MAY PROVE TO BE A BIT OF A STRUGGLE, BUT I PROMISE YOU THAT IT WILL GO IN EVENTUALLY! EASE THE BEADS THROUGH THE OPEN ZIP AND MAKE SURE THAT THE CUSHION IS THE RIGHT WAY UP.

Duffel Bag

what you will need...

- 50 x 110cm print cotton duck
- 30cm square striped fabric
- 20cm square red felt
- scraps of green and blue felt
- bondaweb
- 1m thick cotton cord
- matching sewing thread
- sewing kit
- sewing machine

template

Elephant, page 155

SKILL LEVEL

Whether it's sports kit, swimming towels, school books or holiday clothes, busy families always seem to have endless amounts of 'stuff' to move around from place to place. Make everybody's life a little easier with this roomy drawstring duffel, which should appeal to even the coolest kids!

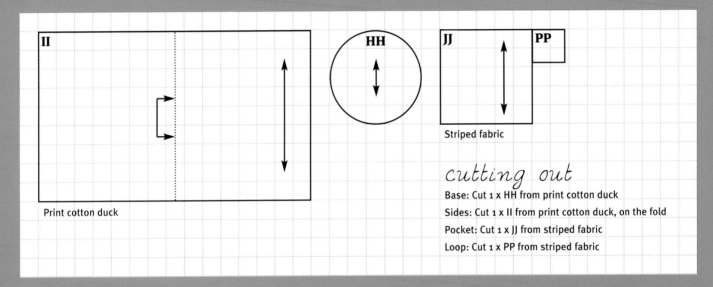

Print cotton duck

Striped fabric

cutting out

Base: Cut 1 x HH from print cotton duck

Sides: Cut 1 x II from print cotton duck, on the fold

Pocket: Cut 1 x JJ from striped fabric

Loop: Cut 1 x PP from striped fabric

The seam allowance throughout is 1.5cm.

1 As shown on page 28, appliqué the felt motif to the pocket and edge the main pieces with satin stitch. I added a green blanket to the basic design, to match those on the 'Circus Elephant' fabric.

2 Sew a 1cm double hem at the top of the pocket, then press under a 1cm turning along the other three edges.

3 Zigzag the sides of the side panel. Sew the completed pocket to the centre, 10cm up from the bottom edge. Reinforce the seams at the top corners with extra stitches.

4 Mark a point 10cm down from the top corner on each side edge. Press a 1cm then a 5cm turning along the top edge. Unfold the second turning and with right sides facing, pin the side edges together from the marked points to the bottom corner. Machine stitch this part of the seam, reinforcing both ends, and press open.

top tip

IF YOU WOULD LIKE TO MAKE A SMALLER VERSION OF THIS BAG, FOR A YOUNGER CHILD PERHAPS, YOU COULD EASILY ADAPT THE BOLSTER CUSHION PATTERN. SHORTEN THE WIDTH OF THE RECTANGLE TO THE HEIGHT REQUIRED, REMEMBERING TO INCLUDE AN EXTRA 6CM FOR THE CASING.

Duffel Bag

5 Refold the second turning and pin it to the top edge of the bag to make the drawstring casing. Machine stitch close to the fold.

6 Fold the loop fabric in half, then press the side edges to the centre crease and top stitch. Fold in half lengthways and stitch both ends to the bottom of the seam, on the right side.

7 Clip the circular base and sides, following the instructions on page 23 and pin together with right sides facing.

8 Seam with two rounds of machine stitch. Trim the allowance back to about 8cm and zigzag to neaten. Turn the bag right side out.

9 Fasten one end of the cord to a safety pin and thread it through the drawstring casing. Take the pin through the loop, then stitch the ends of the cord securely together.

top tip → I DECORATED THE POCKET WITH A BRIGHTLY COLOURED ELEPHANT, TO GO WITH THE FABRIC I CHOSE FOR THE BAGS. IF YOU ARE GOING TO USE A DIFFERENT PRINT YOU COULD SELECT EITHER THE FLOWER, BIRD OR AEROPLANE MOTIFS AS AN ALTERNATIVE.

Shoulder Bag

what you will need...

- 60 x 70cm cotton duck
- matching sewing thread
- 3 2cm buttons
- matching stranded embroidery thread
- sewing kit
- sewing machine

SKILL LEVEL

This versatile little bag is just the right size to carry your essential items, either during the day or for an evening out, and the buttons mean that you can easily adjust the length of the strap. I gave it a slightly more vintage and worn-in look by washing and tumble-drying, to soften up the new fabric.

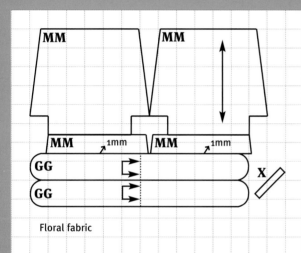

Floral fabric

drawing up the pattern

Facing: Use piece MM, with line 1mm as the bottom edge

cutting out

Front and Back: Cut 2 x MM

Facing: Cut 2

Strap: Cut 2 x GG, on the fold

Button loop: Cut 1 x X, on the bias

The seam allowance throughout is 1cm

1 Zigzag the side and bottom edges of the front and back. Pin, then seam the two pieces together along these edges, with right sides facing.

2 Press the seam allowances open. Join the corners in a 't-junction' as shown on page 22 and neaten the seam allowance. Turn right side out.

3 Make up the button loop, following the rouleau instructions on page 25. Trim it to 8cm and stitch the ends together to form a loop. With raw edges matching and the loop facing downwards, stitch the ends of the rouleau to the centre top of the back, on the right side.

top tip

IF YOU DON'T FANCY MAKING BUTTONHOLES, SIMPLY DECIDE YOUR STRAP LENGTH, THEN SEW THE TWO ENDS DIRECTLY ONTO THE SIDES OF THE BAG. YOU CAN THEN ADD THE BUTTONS AS A DECORATIVE FEATURE.

Shoulder Bag

4 Join the side edges of the facings, with right sides together. Press the seams open and press under a 1cm allowance along the bottom edge.

5 Slip the facing over the top of the bag with right sides together. Line up the side seams, then pin and machine stitch around the top edge. Turn the bag wrong side out.

6 Turn the facing over to the wrong side of the bag and press around the top edge. Tack the bottom edge of the facing to the bag and stitch it down, 3mm from the fold.

7 Top stitch around the opening.

8 Pin tack and stitch the two strap pieces together with right sides facing, leaving an 8cm gap along one edge. Press the seam allowance back on each side of the gap. Notch the seam allowance at the curved ends, as shown on page 23.

9 Turn the strap right side out and ease out the curves. Slip stitch the gap. Press, then top stitch 3mm from the edge. Work two buttonholes at each end, either by hand or machine.

10 Sew one button to the centre front and one to each side seam, positioning them centrally between the two lines of stitching, then button the strap in place.

top tip → YOU COULD GIVE THE BAG A MORE STRUCTURED LOOK BY ADDING A LINING AND A SOLID BASE AS I DID FOR THE SHOPPER BAG VARIATION ON THE NEXT PAGES.

Shopper Bag

SKILL LEVEL

The shoulder bag on the previous pages, which also stars on the front cover of this book, turned out to be such a useful shape and size that I just had to come up with a variation! This rather more structured version has a solid base, a contrasting lining and a shorter, fixed handle made from cotton webbing.

what you will need...

- 45 x 75cm floral print cotton duck
- 35 x 75cm contrasting print for lining
- 10 x 20cm rectangle of thick card
- magnetic bag fastener or large press stud
- 40cm 3cm-wide webbing
- matching sewing thread
- sewing kit
- sewing machine

drawing up the pattern
Facing: Use piece MM with line 1mm as the bottom edge
Tab: Use piece GG with line 2gg as the straight edge

cutting out
Front and Back: Cut 2 x MM from floral print
Facing: Cut 2 from floral print
Tab: Cut 2 from floral print
Lining: Cut 2 x MM from lining print

The seam allowance throughout is 1cm

1 Make up the bag and lining as for the first two steps of the shoulder bag, but don't turn the lining right side out. Place the cardboard at the bottom of the main bag, then slip the lining inside, matching up the side seams.

2 Attach the projecting part of the fastener to the curved end of one tab, on the right side, and 2.5cm up from the end. Tack the second tab on top with right sides facing.

3 Machine stitch around the long and curved edges of the tabs, leaving a 6mm seam allowance. Clip around the curve (see page 23) and turn right side out. Press lightly, avoiding the fastener, and top stitch the seam.

4 Pin the straight end of the tab to the centre top edge of bag, on the right side, with raw edges matching.

5 Pin the webbing centrally to the sides of the bag, so that 3cm at each end projects above the top edge.

6 Make up and sew on the facing as in steps 4 to 6 of the shoulder bag. Work a rectangle of reinforcing stitches across each side seam, as shown on page 26.

7 Fix the recessed part of the fastener to the centre front of the bag, 5cm down from the opening.

8 Finish off the handle by pinning the two edges of the webbing together for 20cm along the centre. Stitch 3mm from the edge.

top tip → YOU WILL NEED TO SEW THROUGH SEVERAL LAYERS OF THICKER FABRIC, PLUS THE COTTON WEBBING, FOR THIS PROJECT. TO MAKE SURE THAT THE STITCHES REMAIN EVEN YOU SHOULD FIT AN EXTRA STRONG NEEDLE TO YOUR SEWING MACHINE.

Large Tote

what you will need...

- 65 x 140cm floral print
- 55 x 85cm spotted fabric
- stranded embroidery thread
- button
- matching sewing thread
- sewing kit
- sewing machine

SKILL LEVEL

This practical tote features my absolute favourite fabric pairing of large-scale roses and spots. It has a useful outside pocket and is roomy enough to carry books and files, or even a laptop, but it would also make a stylish and eco-conscious alternative to plastic carriers when you're out shopping.

Floral Print

Spotted Fabric

cutting out

Front & Back: Cut 2 x NN from floral print

Front Pocket: Cut 1 x N from floral print

Inner Pocket: Cut 1 x JJ from floral print, on the fold

Handles: Cut 2 x GG from floral print, on the fold, following the square corners

Lining: Cut 2 x NN from spotted fabric

top tip → I MADE THE TOTE AND THE LINING FROM COTTON DUCK, WHICH MAKES IT VERY DURABLE, BUT YOU COULD LEAVE OUT THE LINING AND THE INNER POCKET TO MAKE A LIGHTER WEIGHT SHOPPING BAG THAT CAN BE FOLDED UP AND CARRIED IN YOUR HANDBAG.

Large Tote

The seam allowance throughout is 1cm

1 Press under 1cm, then a further 3cm along the top of the front pocket, then top stitch both folds. Make a buttonhole in the centre of the hem.

2 Pin and stitch the pocket to the front bag piece, with raw edges matching. Pin the back of the bag to the front, with right sides together. Machine stitch side and bottom edges. Press under a 1cm, then a 4cm turning around the opening.

3 With right sides facing, sew the side and bottom edges of the two lining pieces together. Press the seam allowances inwards. Trim 5cm off the top edge.

4 Stitch a narrow double hem along one short edge of the inner pocket. With right sides facing, fold in half widthways so that the hem lies 5cm from the other short edge. Pin and seam. Trim the corners, turn right side out and press.

5 Mark a vertical line 7cm in from the right edge and machine along it to divide the pocket. Turn under the unstitched seam allowance at the top corners and slip stitch it down.

6 Pin the top edge of the pocket to the top of the lining, centring it on the back edge. Slip the lining inside the bag and fold the turning over to conceal the raw edges.

7 Make up the handles, neatening the short ends, as shown on page 27. Pin and tack the ends of one handle to the inside back of the bag, so that the edges line up with the pocket. Tack the other handle in the corresponding position on the front.

8 Work a round of stitching 6mm down from the top edge, then a second round, 3cm from the top edge. Work reinforcing stitching over the ends of the handles, as shown on page 26.

9 Finish off by sewing the button to the front of the bag, directly behind the buttonhole.

top tip → YOU CAN ADJUST THE STITCH LINE ON THE INNER POCKET SO THAT YOU HAVE A PERFECT FIT FOR YOUR PHONE AND PURSE, OR MAYBE ADD A NARROW CHANNEL FOR A PEN OR PENCIL.

Inside-out Tote

what you will need...

- 75 x 140cm cotton duck
- 15 x 65cm spotted fabric
- 60cm 2.5cm wide webbing
- 2m bias binding (optional)
- matching sewing thread
- sewing kit
- sewing machine

SKILL LEVEL

This ingenious folding bag is designed with two sets of handles, one in the usual place at the top, and a second pair positioned half-way down the sides. Fold the upper half of the bag to the inside if you just need the standard shopper shown opposite, or open it out completely for bulk purchases – see overleaf!

drawing up the pattern

Front & Back: Use piece P cut on the fold. Trace PP onto each bottom corner, then cut away the marked square

cutting out

Front & Back: Cut 2 from main fabric

Lower Handles: Cut 2 x Q + 10cm on length from main fabric

Border: Cut 2 x L from green spot, on the fold

I BOUND THE INSIDE SEAMS WITH BIAS TAPE TO GIVE THEM EXTRA STRENGTH, BUT YOU COULD ALSO FINISH THEM WITH A ZIGZAG OR OVERLOCKED STITCH SO THAT THEY WILL NOT FRAY.

Inside-out Tote

The seam allowance throughout is 1cm

1 Fold and press a turning 30cm down from the top edge of the front and back pieces to mark the positions for the lower handles.

2 Make up the two lower handles as shown on page 27, then trim each one to 65cm.

3 Position one handle across the front of the bag so that the top edge lies along the crease. Pin the two ends to the side edges of the bag then pin down a 22cm length at the left and right, leaving a 21cm unattached length in the centre.

4 Mark a 3cm rectangle at each end of the unstitched part. Top stitch the top and bottom edges of the pinned parts of the handle and work reinforcing stitching (see page 26) within the rectangles. Do the same on the back of the bag.

5 With right sides facing, pin and stitch the front and back together along the side and bottom edges, leaving the cut out corners free. Bind or overlock the seam allowances.

6 Join the corners with a t-junction seam, as explained on page 22. Fold one seam allowance to the left and one to the right at the point where the two lines of stitching meet, so that you do not have a bulky join.

7 Pin and stitch the ends of the two border strips together, with right sides facing. Press the seams open and press a 1cm turning around one edge.

8 Matching the seams, pin the border around the top edge of the bag, so that the right side faces the wrong side of the bag and the raw edges are aligned.

9 Cut the webbing in half to make two 30cm handles. Measure a point 22cm in from each top corner. Slip the ends of the handles under the border at these points: the ends should project above the top edge for 2cm. Tack the handles securely in place.

10 Turn the bag right side out and fold the border over. Tack down the folded edge, then top stitch both this and the top edge. Work rectangular reinforcing stitches over each end of the handle.

top tip → WHEN THE BAG WAS COMPLETE, I ONCE AGAIN DID MY SPECIAL TRICK OF WASHING IT ON A HOT CYCLE AND THEN TUMBLING UNTIL DRY, TO CREATE A SOFTER, MORE RELAXED APPEARANCE.

Quilted Purse

SKILL LEVEL

The appeal of this project lies in the combination of carefully thought out details: the scalloped edge of the yellow ricrac insertion; the lines of pink quilting stitches; the hand-stitched buttonhole loop and the subtle gleam of a pearl button.

what you will need...

- 55 x 35cm floral print
- 55 x 35cm cotton batting
- 55 x 35cm plain fabric
- 35cm ricrac
- large button
- matching stranded embroidery thread
- pencil and clear ruler
- matching sewing thread
- contrasting sewing thread for quilting
- sewing kit
- sewing machine

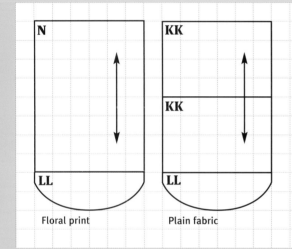

cutting out

Front & Back: Cut 1 x N from floral print

Flap: Cut 1 x LL from floral print

Bag lining: Cut 2 x KK from plain fabric, following square corners

Flap lining: Cut 1 x LL from plain fabric

The seam allowance throughout is 6mm

1 Mark the quilting lines on the main bag and the flap by ruling a diagonal grid of 2.5cm squares on the right side of each piece.

2 Trim 6mm from each side of the flap pattern, then cut a piece of batting to this size. Tack the batting centrally to the wrong side of the flap and quilt the marked lines.

3 Tack a length of ricrac around the flap, so that the edge of the braid lies along the curved edge. Pin the flap lining to the right side of the flap.

top tip →

IF YOUR FABRIC HAS AN OBVIOUSLY DIRECTIONAL DESIGN, CUT THE FRONT AND BACK PIECE WITH THE DESIGN RUNNING LENGTHWAYS. MAKE SURE THAT YOU SEW THE FLAP ONTO THE CORRECT END, OR THE PATTERN WILL APPEAR UPSIDE DOWN ON THE FRONT OF THE BA

Quilted Purse

4 Machine stitch along the curved edge. Clip the seam allowance (see page 23) and turn right side out. Ease out the curves and press lightly.

5 Quilt the front and back piece of the bag as for the flap. With right sides facing, pin and stitch the straight edge of the flap to the top back edge of the bag.

6 Fold the bag in half lengthways with wrong sides facing and tuck the flap inside. Pin and stitch the side seams.

7 Stitch the two bag lining pieces together along the side edges. Press the seam allowances inwards, then press in a 1cm turning along the bottom edges. Turn right side out.

8 Slip the lining inside the bag so the right sides are facing and the seams aligned. Pin the top edges together so that the flap is sandwiched between the two. Machine stitch all around the opening.

9 Turn the bag right sides out through the opening and ease it into shape. Close the gap in the lining with slip stitch.

10 Work a buttonhole loop at the edge of the flap and sew the button to the front of the bag, in line with the loop.

top tip

I CHOSE A CLASSIC GRID PATTERN FOR THE HAND-QUILTING, THE SAME AS I USED ON THE HOTTIE. YOU COULD VARY THE STITCH PATTERN, DEPENDING ON YOUR FABRIC: IF YOU'RE WORKING WITH STRIPED FABRIC, FOR EXAMPLE, TRY QUILTING ALONG THE PARALLEL LINES.

T-Junction Washbag

what you will need...

- 30 x 80cm cotton fabric
- 30 x 65cm shower curtain fabric
- 40cm nylon zip
- 70cm bias binding
- 10 x 20cm medium weight iron-on interfacing
- matching sewing thread
- sewing kit
- sewing machine

SKILL LEVEL

I have always enjoyed finding new and unexpected uses for old fabrics, and this zip-up washbag started its life as a fifties sundress with a flouncy skirt! The wide turquoise and white stripes of the soft cotton are just perfect for the structured shape, which is finished off at the corners with t-junction seams.

Striped Fabric

Interfacing

Waterproof Fabric

drawing up the pattern

Side: Use piece KK, tracing around the entire outline and following the square corners. Add flap LL to the top edge.

cutting out

Bag: Cut two sides from cotton fabric
Lining: Cut two sides from waterproof fabric
Tabs: Cut 4 x OO from interfacing

1 Tack the lining pieces to the wrong side of the bag pieces, around all four edges.

2 Open out the zip and pin one straight edge along one curved edge of the bag, with right sides together. The zip is longer than the bag, so leave an equal overlap at each end.

3 Fit a zip foot to the machine and stitch down, 5mm from the teeth. Do the same at the other side. Press the seams outwards and top stitch, close to the stitch lines.

4 With right sides facing, pin and stitch the side and bottom edges together through all four layers. Leave 1cm unstitched at each top corner.

5 Join the bottom corners with a 't-junction seam' as shown on page 22. Turn right side out and slip the ends of the zip through the gaps at the top of the side seams. Slip stitch to close. Trim and bind the inside seams.

6 Iron the tabs onto the remaining fabric and cut out, leaving a 6mm margin all round. Tack this to the back, then slip stitch the tabs together in pairs, around the side and bottom edges. Trim the ends of the zip to 2cm and ease them through the top of the tabs. Stitch in place.

top tip →

IF, LIKE ME, YOU CHOOSE STRIPES, YOU WILL NEED TO ALLOW A LITTLE EXTRA FABRIC SO THAT EVERYTHING MATCHES. MAKE SURE THE DESIGN LINES UP ON FRONT AND BACK, AND CUT FOUR IDENTICAL TABS WITH THE STRIPES RUNNING HORIZONTALLY.

Drawstring Washbag

what you will need...

- 60 x 80cm patterned cotton fabric
- 35 x 45cm waterproof fabric
- 70cm fine piping cord
- 70cm contrast bias binding
- 70cm white bias binding
- matching sewing thread
- ruler
- sewing kit
- sewing machine

SKILL LEVEL

Here's another quirky recycled dress fabric – this time a painterly Sixties pattern of brightly coloured squares. I found a length of bias tape that proved to be the perfect match for the vivid green and used this to bind the main seam. The drawstring cords are made from two long rouleaux, cut from the main fabric.

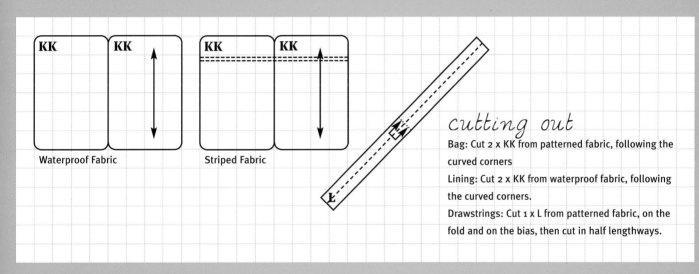

Waterproof Fabric

Striped Fabric

cutting out

Bag: Cut 2 x KK from patterned fabric, following the curved corners

Lining: Cut 2 x KK from waterproof fabric, following the curved corners.

Drawstrings: Cut 1 x L from patterned fabric, on the fold and on the bias, then cut in half lengthways.

1 Mark two points on each side, 6 and 7cm down from the top edge of one bag piece. Using a fading pen, rule between both sets of points, so that you have two parallel lines across the right side.

2 Pin the top part of the bag piece to a lining piece, with right sides facing. Leaving a 1cm allowance, machine stitch around the top edge between the upper two points, reinforcing both ends of the stitching.

3 Make a 1cm snip into both layers of fabric, at the ends of the lower line. Clip the corners, press the seam allowances inwards and turn right side out.

THIS PROJECT INTRODUCES YOU TO PIPED SEAMS AND ROULEAUX TIES – TWO SLIGHTLY MORE ADVANCED TECHNIQUES THAT ARE MUCH USED IN DRESSMAKING AND SOFT FURNISHINGS. DON'T BE PUT OFF HOWEVER, AS THE BAG IS NOT NEARLY AS TRICKY AS IT MAY LOOK AT FIRST!

Drawstring Washbag

4 Machine stitch along both lines to make the drawstring channel, then make up the second side in the same way.

5 Cover the piping cord with the contrast bias binding, as shown on page 23. With raw edges matching and an overlap of about 3cm at each end, pin the piping to the right side of one bag piece. Fold the loose cord outwards at an angle.

6 Tack the second side to the first, with right sides facing.

7 Fit the zip foot to your machine and sew the two sides together, close to the edge of the cord. Stitch over the angled ends of the piping. Trim the piping and clip corners.

8 Neaten the seam allowance by covering it with the white bias binding, then turn right side out and press lightly.

9 Make up the two drawstrings as shown on page 25. Fasten a small safety pin to the first one and pass it through the gap between the two lines of stitching and along the drawstring channels on the front and back of the bag. Thread the second rouleau from the other side. Knot the ends of both cords and trim.

top tip

THE DRAWSTRINGS ARE MADE FROM VERY NARROW TUBES OF FABRIC: IF YOUR CHOSEN MATERIAL IS TOO THICK YOU WILL NOT BE ABLE TO DRAW IT THROUGH TO MAKE THE ROULEAUX, SO LOOK OUT FOR A FINE MATCHING COTTON INSTEAD. YOU COULD ALSO USE THIS FOR THE PIPING.

Jewellery Roll

what you will need...

- 25 x 80cm cotton duck
- 20cm nylon zip
- 1.5m bias binding
- 1 medium press stud
- 50cm fine piping cord
- matching sewing thread
- sewing kit
- sewing machine

SKILL LEVEL

Keep all your bracelets, necklaces and brooches safe when you're out and about, by tucking them into the various compartments of this practical jewellery holder, then slide your rings onto the fabric tube. This project would make a great gift for all ages. It is perfect to take travelling or keep your precious jewels tucked away in a drawer.

Cotton duck

drawing up the pattern

Inside: Use piece KK, following the curved corners at the left edge. Cut along line 1kk so you have two pieces.

Outside: Use piece KK, following the square corners at the right edge. Trim 4cm from the left edge.

cutting out

Inside: Cut both parts from main fabric

Outside: Cut 1 from main fabric

Pockets: Cut 2 x PP from main fabric

Ring Holder: Cut 1 x PP from main fabric, on the fold

top tip → IF YOU WANT TO MAKE A MORE PADDED JEWELLERY ROLL YOU COULD SANDWICH A LAYER OF COTTON OR POLYESTER WADDING BETWEEN THE INSIDE AND OUTSIDE PIECES.

Jewellery Roll

1 Press under a 2cm turning along the right edge of the narrow inside piece and the left edge of the wide piece. Sew the zip between these folded edges (see page 25) and trim the projecting ends.

2 Stitch a narrow hem along one edge of each pocket and press a 6mm turning under the other three edges. With the hems on the left, pin them both to the right hand side of the inside piece, 2cm from the edges. Machine stitch down, close to the folds. Close the zip.

3 Press a 1cm turning along one long edge of the ring holder. Starting at the opposite edge, roll it up tightly with the right side outwards. Pin, then stitch down the fold. Neaten one end, with the seam at the back. Sew the projecting part of the press stud across the seam, 1cm up from the bottom edge.

4 Flatten out the open end of the ring holder. Pin, then stitch it securely to the top edge of the inside piece, 7cm to the right of the zip. Sew the second part of the press stud to the lower edge of the inside, in line with the first part.

5 Pin the outside piece to the completed inside with wrong sides facing and trim to the same width. Machine stitch 6mm from the outer edge. Trim the seam allowance back to 3mm.

6 Using a fading pen, rule a line across the inside, 1cm to the right of the ring holder. Machine stitch along this line.

7 Starting at the centre left, neaten the outside edge with bias binding, stitching it down by hand or machine. Ease the folded edges round the curved corners, stretching it gently. Turn the binding under at a 45 degree angle at the square corners.

8 For the tie, cover the piping cord with the rest of the bias binding. Press under 1cm at one end, then wrap the binding over the cord. Slip stitch the folded edges together, neatening the other end in the same way. Fold the tie in half to find the centre and stitch this point securely to the centre left edge.

Specs Case

what you will need...

- 35 x 25cm printed fabric
- 35 x 50cm velvet
- 25 x 35cm cotton batting
- 75cm fine piping cord
- small button
- matching sewing thread
- matching stranded embroidery cotton
- sewing kit
- sewing machine

SKILL LEVEL

A round of vibrant pink piping gives a new twist to this classic spectacle case, and shows how you can transform an everyday item into something really individual by changing just one small design element. The case has a soft velvet lining and an inner padded layer to protect your specs or sunglasses.

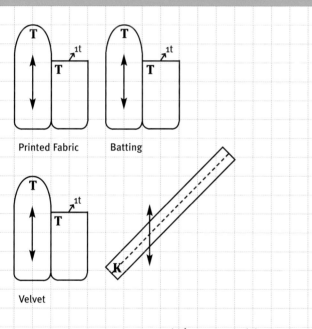

Printed Fabric   Batting

Velvet

drawing up the pattern
Front: Use piece T, with line 1t as the top edge and following the curved corners

cutting out
Back: Cut 1 x T from printed fabric, following the curved corners

Front: Cut 1 from printed fabric

Back Lining: Cut 1 x T from velvet

Front Lining: Cut 1 front from velvet

Piping: Cut 1 x K from velvet, on the bias, then cut in half lengthways

Batting: Cut one front and one back

1 Join the two bias strips, as shown on page 21 and use it to cover the piping cord (see page 23). Matching the raw edges, tack the piping around the outside edge of the back piece, starting at the centre bottom edge. Cross the two ends over where they meet, and trim the overlap.

top tip →

THE VELVET PIPING HAS A GRAPHIC QUALITY, WHICH EMPHASISES THE OUTLINE OF THE CASE. THE BRIGHT PINK VELVET REALLY MAKES IT STAND OUT AGAINST THE GENTLE DOVE GREY BACKGROUND, SO PICK A STRONG COLOUR FROM YOUR MAIN FABRIC TO ACHIEVE THE SAME EFFECT.

Specs Case

2 Press a 1cm turning along the top edge of the front piece. With right sides facing, pin and tack the front to the back around the side and bottom edges. Fit a zip foot and stitch together. Trim the seam allowance to 6mm, clip the corners and turn right side out.

3 Trim away a margin of 1cm all around the outside edges of the front and back pattern pieces and use these as a guide to cut the batting. Tack the back batting centrally to the wrong side of the back lining, so there is a 1cm allowance all round.

4 Press a 1cm turning along the top edge of the front lining. Pin the batting to the wrong side, leaving a 1cm allowance all round. Fold the turning over the batting and tack.

5 With right sides together, pin, tack and machine stitch the front and back lining pieces together, leaving a 1cm seam allowance.

6 Trim the seam allowance on the side and bottom edges of the lining to 4mm.

7 Fold the surplus lining around the flap to the back of the batting, pleating it a little as you go around the curve, and tack it down.

8 Slip the finished lining inside the case, so the wrong sides are together. Ease the corners of the lining into place.

9 Slip stitch the top straight edge of the front to the top of the lining. Tack the flap lining back on to the flap and slip stitch it down around the curved edge, next to the piping.

10 Work a buttonhole stitch loop at the centre edge of the flap as shown on page 25. Sew a button to the front of the completed case, in line with the loop.

top → *tip*

THE HANDMADE BUTTONHOLE LOOP, IN THE SAME GREY AS THE MAIN FABRIC, IS A WONDERFUL FINISHING TOUCH. IT IS NOT DIFFICULT TO DO, BUT IF YOU HAVEN'T USED THIS STITCH BEFORE, IT'S WORTH TAKING TIME TO PRACTISE THE TECHNIQUE ON A PIECE OF SPARE FABRIC.

iPod® Case

SKILL LEVEL

Traditional sewing techniques and the newest technology come together in this sweet little padded bag – the perfect safe home for your mobile phone or MP3 player. The drawstring fastening is made from nylon cord and secured with a spring toggle, which you can find at any good haberdashers.

cutting out

Bag: Cut 1 x CC from printed fabric

Tabs: Cut 4 x OO from printed fabric

Lining: Cut 1 x CC from brushed cotton

Padding: Cut 1 x CC from cotton batting

1 Fold the bag in half with right sides facing. Pin, then seam the side and bottom edges together, leaving a 1cm allowance.

2 Press open the top 6cm of the side seam. Press a 2.5cm turning around the top edge, then turn the bag right side out.

3 Press a 2.5cm turning at each end of the bias tape, then press it in half lengthways with the turnings on the inside.

4 Tack the tape around the bag opening, with raw edges on the inside and 6mm of the folded edge projecting above the top edge. Line folded ends of the tape up with the side seam.

5 Pin the lining to the padding and make up as in step 1. Press the seam allowances inwards, then press a 2.5cm turning around the top edge. Slip the lining inside the bag, positioning it so that the side seam is opposite the opening.

6 Tack the top edge of the lining to the top edge of the bag, stitching through the tape. Slip stitch the edges together.

7 Fasten a safety pin to one end of the cord and thread it through the tape channel. Slip two ends through the toggle.

8 Press under a 1cm turning along each tab piece, straightening off the curve at the bottom edges. Pin together in pairs and slip stitch the side and bottom edges. Push the ends of the cord through the openings and close with slip stitch.

top tip

I WAS LUCKY ENOUGH TO COME ACROSS A BINDING TAPE IN EXACTLY THE SAME SHADE OF ORANGE AS THE DETAILS ON THE DAISY PETALS, BUT IF YOU CAN'T FIND THE COLOUR YOU'RE LOOKING FOR, YOU CAN SIMPLY CUT A 4CM-WIDE BIAS STRIP FROM PLAIN FABRIC.

Addresses

Haberdasheries and fabric shops

All the Fun of the Fair
Unit 2.8
Kingly Court
Carnaby Street
London
W1B 5PW
020 7287 2303
www.allthefunofthefair.biz

Bedecked
5 Castle Street
Hay-on-Wye
HR3 5DF
01497 822769
www.bedecked.co.uk

Creative Quilting
32 Bridge Road
East Molesey
KT8 9HA
020 8941 7075
www.creativequilting.co.uk

Harts of Hertford
14 Bull Plain
Hertford
SG14 1DT
01992 558106
www.hartsofhertford.com

John Lewis
Oxford Street
London
W1A 1EX
and branches nationwide
08456 049049
www.johnlewis.com

Mandors
134 Renfrew Street
Glasgow
G3 6ST
0141 332 7716
www.mandors.co.uk

MacCulloch & Wallis
25–26 Dering Street
London
W1S 1AT
020 7629 0311
www.macculloch-wallis.co.uk

Millie Moon
20 Paul Street
Frome
Somerset
BA11 1DT
01373 464650
www.milliemoonshop.co.uk

Peabees Patchwork Bazaar
1 Hare Street
Sheerness
Kent
ME12 1AH
01795 669963
www.peabees.com

Rags
19 Chapel Walk
Crowngate Shopping Centre
Worcester
WR1 3LD
01905 612330

Sew and So's
14 Upper Olland Street
Bungay
Suffolk
NR35 1BG
01986 896147
www.sewandsos.co.uk

Tikki
293 Sandycombe Road
Kew
Surrey
TW9 3LU
020 8948 8462
www.tikkilondon.com

Addresses

Sewing Classes

Alison Victoria School of Sewing
71 Market Street
Ashby de la Zouch
Leicestershire LE65 1AH
www.schoolofsewing.co.uk

Liberty Sewing School
Regent Street
London W1B 5AH
www.liberty.co.uk

Modern Approach Sewing School
Astra Business Centre
Roman Way
Ribbleton
Preston PR2 5AP
01772 498862
www.sewjanetmoville.co.uk

Sue Hazell Sewing Tuition
Southcombe House
Chipping Norton
Oxfordshire OX7 5QH
www.sewing-tuition.co.uk

The Studio London
Studio 5
Trinity Buoy Wharf
64 Orchard Place
London E14 0JW
www.thestudiolondon.co.uk

Fairs

Great Northern Contemporary Craft Fair
Spinningfields
Manchester
www.greatnorthernevents.co.uk

Knitting and Stitching Show
Alexandra Palace
London and
RDS
Dublin and
Harrogate International Centre
01473 320407
www.twistedthread.com

Sewing for Pleasure
NEC
Birmingham
www.ichf.co.uk

A few handy websites:

DMC
www.dmccreative.co.uk
Sewing and embroidery threads.

Donna Flower
www.donnaflower.com
Online store of both antique
and vintage fabrics.

Etsy
www.etsy.com
An online marketplace for everything
handmade and vintage, including
fabric and other sewing supplies.

Fabric Rehab
www.fabricrehab.co.uk
For vintage and contemporary prints.

Ribbon Moon
www.ribbonmoon.co.uk
For ricrac and bias binding in a
wide range of colours and widths.

So Vintage Patterns
www.sovintagepatterns.com
For a collection of over 4,000 vintage
sewing patterns.

Vintage Fabric Market
www.vintagefabricmarket.co.uk
For antique fabrics, accessories
and other collectables.

Addresses

Cath Kidston's shops

Bath
3 Broad Street
Milsom Place
Bath BA1 5LJ
01225 331 006

Brighton
31a & 32 East Street
Brighton BN1 1HL
01273 227 420

Bristol
79 Park Street
Clifton
Bristol BS1 5PF
0117 930 4722

Cambridge
31 Market Hill
Cambridge CB2 3NU
01223 351 810

Cheltenham
21 The Promenade
Cheltenham GL50 1LE
01242 245 912

Chichester
24 South Street
Chichester PO19 1EL
01243 850 100

Dublin
Unit CSD 1.3
Dundrum Shopping Centre
Dublin 16
01 296 4430

Edinburgh
58 George Street
Edinburgh EH2 2LR
0131 220 1509

Guildford
14–18 Chertsey Street
Guildford GU1 4HD
01483 564 798

Harrogate
4–6 James Street
Harrogate HG1 1RF
01423 531 481

Kildare
Unit 21c Kildare Village
Nurney Road
Kildare Town
00 353 45 535 084

Kingston
10 Thames Street
Kingston upon Thames KT1 1PE
020 8546 6760

Leeds
26 Lands Lane
Leeds LS1 6LB
0113 397 1330

Liverpool
Compton House
18 School Lane
Liverpool L1 3BT
0151 709 2747

London – Battersea
142 Northcote Road
Battersea
London SW11 6RD
020 7228 6571

London – Chiswick
125 Chiswick High Road
Chiswick
London W4 2ED
020 8995 8052

London – Covent Garden
28–32 Shelton Street
Covent Garden
London WC2H 9JE
020 7836 4803

London – Fulham
668 Fulham Road
Fulham
London SW6 5RX
020 7731 6531

Addresses

London – Heathrow Terminal 4
Departure Lounge
Heathrow Airport
Hounslow TW6 3XA
020 8759 5578

London – Kings Road
322 Kings Road
Chelsea
London SW3 5UH
020 7351 7335

London – Marylebone
51 Marylebone High Street
Marylebone
London W1U 5HW
020 7935 6555

London – Notting Hill
158 Portobello Road
Notting Hill
London W11 2BE
020 7727 5278

London – Sloane Square
27 Kings Road
Chelsea
London SW3 4RP
020 3463 4840

Marlow
6 Market Square
Marlow SL7 1DA
01628 484 443

Oxford
6 Broad Street
Oxford OX1 3AJ
01865 791 576

Portsmouth
Gunwharf Quays
Portsmouth PO1 3TU
02392 832 982

St Ives
67 Fore Street
St Ives TR26 1HE
01736 798 001

Tunbridge Wells
59–61 High Street
Tunbridge Wells TN1 1XU
01892 521 197

Wimbledon Village
3 High Street
Wimbledon SW19 5DX
020 8944 1001

Winchester
46 High Street
Winchester SO23 9BT
01962 870 620

Windsor
24 High Street
Windsor SL4 1LH
01753 830 591

York
32 Stonegate
York YO1 8AS
01904 733 653

Concessions in:
Bicester Village (outlet store), Oxfordshire-
Selfridges, The Bull Ring, Birmingham
Selfridges, Oxford Street, London
Selfridges, Exchange Square, Manchester
Selfridges, Trafford Centre, Manchester
Fenwicks, Northumberland Street,
Newcastle Upon Tyne

Acknowledgments

Many thanks to Lucinda Ganderton and Jess Pemberton for making all of the projects, Pia Tryde, Laura Mackay, Bridget Bodoano and Elaine Ashton. Thanks also to Katherine Case, Lisa Pendreigh and Helen Lewis at Quadrille.

Cath Kidston

Editorial Director: Anne Furniss
Art Director: Helen Lewis
Project Editor: Lisa Pendreigh
Designer: Katherine Case
Photographer: Pia Tryde
Illustrator: Bridget Bodoano
Design Assistant to Cath Kidston:
Laura Mackay
Project Maker and Sewing Consultant:
Lucinda Ganderton
Sewing Assistants: Jessica Pemberton
and Lis Gunner
Production Director: Vincent Smith
Production Controller: Aysun Hughes

This edition was first published in 2011 by
Quadrille Publishing Limited
Alhambra House
27–31 Charing Cross Road
London WC2H 0LS
www.quadrille.co.uk

Cataloguing-in-Publication Data: a catalogue record for this book is available from the British Library.

ISBN 978 184949 062 7

Printed in China

Templates

Elephant Template
needed for:
Cot Quilt pp100–103
Duffel Bag pp112–115

Hexagon Template
needed for:
Knitting Bag pp80-83

Heart Template
needed for:
Heart Teatowel pp52–53
Birdie Tablecloth pp58–59
Lavender Bags pp64–65
Pincushion pp76–79
Girl's Apron pp88–89
Heart Quilt pp104–107

Bird Template
needed for:
Bird Cushion pp38–41
Birdie Tablecloth pp58–59
Lavender Bags pp64–65
Bird Mobile pp94–97
Cot Quilt pp100–103

Aeroplane Template
needed for:
Aeroplane Blanket
pp108–109

Flower Template
needed for:
Flower Cushion pp46–47
Heart Quilt pp104–107

Stanley Template
needed for:
Stanley Picture pp92–93
Stanley Toy pp98–99